SOUTH SUSSEX

35 downland and coastal walks
around
BRIGHTON and WORTHING

COLIN ULPH

with sketch maps and line drawings by the author

COLIN ULPH * SHOREHAM BY SEA * 1995

While every care has been taken in compiling this book, the author cannot accept responsibility for inaccuracies such as removal of gates and stiles or the ploughing of paths. At the time of publication all of the routes are along public rights of way or other paths over which the public has undisputed access. Please report any obstruction to the highway authority so that the way may be cleared for others. Please also note that all car parking is entirely at the owner's risk.

Ordnance Survey maps covering the routes:

> 1:50000 Landranger series (approx 1¼ in to 1 mile):
>> Sheets 197 and 198
> 1:25000 Pathfinder series (approx 2½ in to 1 mile):
>> Sheets 1287, 1288, 1306, 1307 and 1308.

British Library Cataloguing in Publication Data.
A catalogue record for this book is available from the British Library

© 1995   Colin Ulph

ISBN 0 9511088 2 4

Colin Ulph, Coombes, 281 Upper Shoreham Road, Shoreham by Sea, West Sussex BN43 6BB.

Produced by **Kensett Ltd, 196 Old Shoreham Road, Hove, East Sussex BN3 7EH.**

INDEX

The Saxon church of St Mary the Virgin, Sompting *(Walk 11)*

4

PREFACE

Those of us who live between the Sussex downs and the sea are really fortunate to have such lovely countryside right on our doorstep. The downs provide us with bracing walks in delightful surroundings, protect us from the worst of the winter weather, and restrict the spread of the coastal towns into the countryside through their status as an Area of Outstanding Beauty - and perhaps, one day, a National Park.

The purpose of *South Sussex Rambles* - apart from giving me an excuse to spend a winter walking the downs - is two-fold. I want to help local people and visitors to enjoy the many delights of our local countryside, but I also have the long-term aim of keeping paths open for future generations by making sure that they are well used NOW.

So what will you see on a downland walk? Hillforts, and countless other traces of the people who lived on the downs in prehistoric times; ancient parish churches of all shapes and sizes - a tribute to the inspiration, faith and skill of our Saxon and Norman ancestors; remote, picturesque villages with flint-walled cottages, thatched roofs and cosy little pubs; castles and windmills; springs and dewponds; birds, butterflies and tiny, colourful, low-growing plants that thrive on the thin soil of chalk hills - the list is almost endless. When you are on the downs, there is also that wonderful sense of space that seems incredible only a mile or so from one of the most populous parts of the British coast.

South Sussex Rambles covers much the same area as its predecessor *Southdown Walks*, but I have widened the boundaries to include the banks of the rivers Arun in the west and Ouse in the east, as well as some of the less spoiled parts of our coastline.

Here are just a few things to remember while using the book.

- 1. The maps are only sketch maps, with just sufficient detail for you to follow the route on an Ordnance Survey map.

- 2. Some features in the countryside do change: gates, fences or even trig points might disappear the day after I wrote about them, so allow for that possibility.

- 3. The hilltop views I have described may be restricted if the weather is less than clear.

- 4. You will not find all the churches open - a sad reality of life today.

- 5. This is Sussex, so there will be mud - even in a dry spell - especially on bridleways and in fields around farm gates. So be prepared, and wear sturdy, waterproof footwear.

I hope that this book, like its predecessors, will guide you to new and fascinating corners of the Sussex downs, and that you will be encouraged to learn more about their history, geography and wildlife. I hope, too, that you will want to use your map to try some of the other hundreds of paths that could not be fitted into a small book like this.

So off you go. Remember to take your camera or sketch pad to capture the enjoyment of the day. Remember, too, to take that most important thing, your TIME, to savour to the full the true magic of the Sussex downs.

I have had a wonderful winter preparing this book. I hope you enjoy using it.

COLIN ULPH
April 1995

THE ROUTES

THE AREA

A key to the area covered by each walk

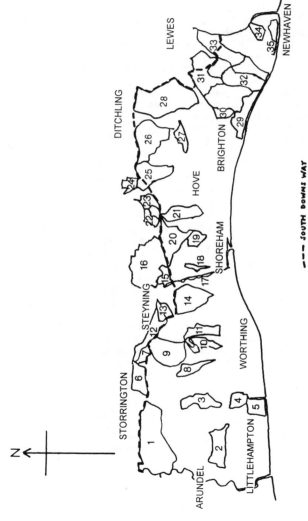

SELECTING A WALK

The routes in this book cater for a wide variety of tastes. Here is a list that may help you to select one that meets yours.

Longer walks (10-13 miles)	*1, 12, 16, 17, 20, 25, 28, 31*
Short walks (2½-5 miles)	*4, 5, 7, 8, 10, 13, 18, 19, 22, 24, 27, 30, 34*
Climbing 1000ft or more	*1, 11, 20, 25, 26, 31*
Climbing 250ft or less	*2, 4, 5, 17, 18*
South Downs Way	*1, 6, 7, 9, 12, 13, 14, 15, 16, 20, 23, 25, 26, 28, 31, 33*
Downs Link and Coastal Link	*16, 17*
River banks	*1, 4, 5, 15, 16, 17, 33, 34*
Woodland sections	*2, 7, 11, 12, 13, 22, 23, 26, 27*
Disused railway tracks	*16, 17, 21*
Ancient churches	*1, 2, 3, 6, 8, 11, 13, 14, 15, 16, 17, 21, 22, 23, 24, 25, 26, 28, 29, 30, 31, 32, 34, 35*
Windmills	*4, 8, 24, 25, 26, 29, 30, 32*
Castles	*1, 2, 16, 17*
Hillforts	*4, 7, 9, 10, 11, 12, 20, 21, 22, 23, 24, 25, 26, 27*
Ponds and lakes	*3, 7, 9, 12, 14, 21, 23, 25, 26, 32*
Seaside	*5, 29, 32, 33, 35*
Food & drink at about half way	*1, 2, 5, 8, 11, 12, 16, 17, 20, 21, 22, 28, 29, 31, 33, 34, 35*

MAP FOR WALK 1
(OS Pathfinder maps 1287 and 1306)

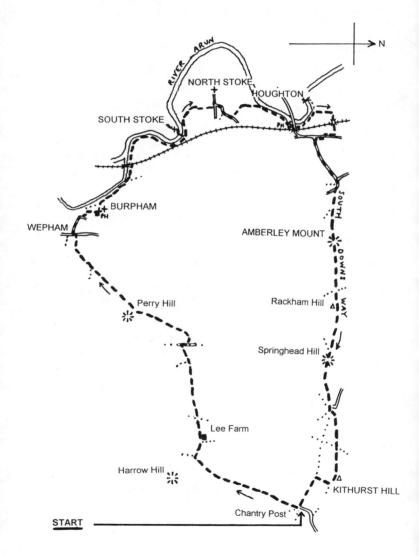

Walk 1

BURPHAM AND THE ARUN

Chantry Post - Lee Farm - Perry Hill - Wepham - Burpham -
South Stoke - North Stoke - Houghton bridge - Amberley
Mount - Rackham Hill - Springhead Hill - Kithurst Hill -
Chantry Post

The first walk in the book is one of the best, but not one to attempt until you are reasonably fit! You will visit three ancient churches, see two medieval castles, and enjoy some truly unspoiled countryside. The walk includes nearly three miles along the banks of the Arun and five miles on the South Downs Way. The going is generally firm, although the meadows around the Arun are liable to flooding in the monsoon season. There are pubs at Burpham and Houghton bridge.

Distance 13 miles   **Climbing** 1130 ft **Highest point** 700ft

Start in the car park at Chantry Post, on the top of the downs south of STORRINGTON (*map ref TQ 087119*). You get to it from A283 by Chantry Lane, a steep, winding, two-mile single-track road - alive with rabbits and pheasants.

Go through the gate on the South Downs Way south of the car park and walk south on the well-defined path towards the domed shape of Harrow Hill, site of over a hundred prehistoric flint mines. As you go, a line of hills appears L - Cissbury Ring (farthest), Church Hill (near Findon), Blackpatch Hill and (nearest the sea) Highdown Hill. Just below Harrow Hill the path veers R and descends to Lee Farm.

Head west through the farm on a concrete lane and then continue in the same direction on a broad, firm track. At the top of a small rise, when the downs on the west side of the Arun come into view, turn R on a short stretch of concrete road, and in 20 yards fork L on a track that curves L to head west and then south. Soon a south view unfolds that includes Bognor Regis, Arundel and the distant Isle of Wight.

Continue to walk south over the top of Perry Hill, passing close to a group of trees L called Norfolk Clump. Once over the summit the path veers south-west and gently descends above the village of Burpham, R. When a footpath joins L, turn R just above the village and then follow the path that turns to the south-west again, now dropping more steeply in the direction of Arundel Castle.

Arriving on a lane in the hamlet of WEPHAM, turn L for 50 yards and then go R along an attractive lane heading for Burpham. Cross a stream and at a sharp R turn in the road find a footpath straight ahead that climbs a steep bank and emerges on a large, grassy plateau surrounded by trees. This is The Burgh, the site of a Saxon fortified township. Go west across the field and turn R towards the church. Pass the cricket pavilion R and emerge in a small square where you will find Burpham House, the George & Dragon pub and a twitten leading to the church of St Mary the Virgin, BURPHAM.

The church dates from Saxon times, but is mainly early 12th century. It is a cruciform building, but the solid 15th century tower stands at the western end and not in the middle. Among the best features in a rather dark interior are the Norman arches into the two transepts and the vaulted 13th century ceiling of the chancel.

Go back down the churchyard path and turn R down the lane, past the forge and by a footpath down to the banks of a reeded ox-bow lake formed by one of the great meanders of the river Arun. Turn R and walk along the bank, crossing the London-Portsmouth railway line with great care. Just after this the lake joins the main flow of the Arun. Continue to walk along the river bank as it sweeps north, giving superb views across to the hamlet of SOUTH STOKE on its little hill. As the river passes north of the village there is a footbridge that you can cross to climb up the hill and visit the beautiful church of St Leonard.

This building, with its slender tower and distinctive tall cap, was begun by the Normans and modified in the 13th century. The inside is a real delight. It is light, welcoming and a model of simplicity and peace. Watch out for the works of a local poet around the walls.

Go back over the bridge and turn L along the river bank for 150 more yards. Then leave it R by a footpath that stays on a raised bank above the water meadows. After just over ¼ mile a wooden suspension bridge carries your path across a sometimes dried-up stream, and you then continue north up the slope to NORTH STOKE, another hamlet on a small hill above the water meadows. Arriving on a surfaced lane turn L and walk down it to visit another interesting church.

No longer used for worship, North Stoke church was placed in the care of The Churches Conservation Trust in 1992. It has a most unusual, dumpy exterior, with a squat little bell tower inserted half way up the roof of the north transept. Inside, it is light and spacious, with much evidence of Norman and Early English work. It has a simple, Norman font and a 14th century wall painting around the chancel arch.

Walk back up the road and at the junction turn L. Just after passing a row of three flint-faced, tile-hung cottages R, go through a gate L to take another raised footpath that will take you back to the river bank opposite HOUGHTON. Turn R to head north, and just before Houghton's road bridge go over a footbridge to arrive on the road.

Turn R and pass a restaurant, cafe and pub. Before reaching the railway bridge take a footpath L that takes you to the river bank again. When you are in sight of the new bridge that carries the South Downs Way across the Arun, leave the bank for the last time to pick up the Way as it heads north for 200 yards and then bears R to go east. As you go over the railway bridge look L for a good view of Amberley Castle, a mile away to the north.

Reaching the road once more, follow the South Downs Way along its grass verge. Cross the road when indicated, and in another 100 yards turn L up High Titten. A sign here tells you that you are 50 miles from Eastbourne and 51 from Winchester (the two ends of the South Downs Way). Look over a brick wall R for a bird's-eye view of the Chalk Pits

Industrial Museum, which is worth a return visit when you have more time.

In front of 'Highdown' follow the lane R, but in 100 yards leave it to continue on the South Downs Way by a rough track L. Now comes the steep bit, as the Way climbs to the top of AMBERLEY MOUNT for an excellent view across the Arun.

To the south-west you can see Bognor Regis, Arundel Castle and Houghton, with the Isle of Wight on the horizon. West are the villages of Bury and Amberley, the distinctive Bignor Hill (with the masts) and Tegleaze, highest of the Sussex downs. In the north-west is Amberley village, with Blackdown in the distance, while the large town to the north is Pulborough.

Now continue east over Rackham Hill (634ft) and Springhead Hill, with glimpses of Parham's Elizabethan mansion L and the Channel coast R. In the dip where there is a small car park, you have a choice. You may continue along the Way, or for a splendid view of the downs leave it L and in 10 yards go R on a bridleway that climbs to the summit of KITHURST HILL at 700ft.

The north view to Storrington is obscured by trees, but east and west there are extensive views along the downs. In the east the next prominent hill is Chanctonbury, with Wolstonbury on the horizon. To the west the downs roll on to Bignor Hill. You can see the sandy ridges of Sussex and Surrey and the North Downs to the north, and glimpses of the coast around Littlehampton in the south.

From Kithurst, continue to walk east for 100 yards, and then take a bridleway R that will lead you back to the South Downs Way. Now turn L to get back to the car park where you started.

Walk 2

THE COASTAL PLAIN

Angmering - The Dover - Crossbush - Lyminster - Poling - Angmering

A walk that is full of variety and very little climbing. It combines delightful woodland, open meadows, three ancient churches and a pub at half way. Some of the paths are boggy after heavy rain.

Distance 8½ miles   **Climbing** 120ft   **Highest point** 80ft

Start in the centre of ANGMERING village. Park where you can in the area around the Lamb Inn and St Margaret's parish church *(map ref TQ 067044).*

Walk up Arundel Road past St Margaret's church, Rectory Lane and St Wilfrid's Catholic church, all L. Directly after the Catholic church school take a surfaced footpath L that passes a graveyard R and then a playing field L. Soon the path swings north, keeping a modern housing estate R. Notice the extensive view of the flat coastal plain to the west.

Continue north, and just after going through a small wood, pass the handsome brick farmhouse of New Place Farm R. Soon afterwards the path comes out on to the A27 trunk road. Turn L along the roadside path for 150 yards, cross the road with care and resume the walk north up a lane. This will take you through Priorsleas Farm to the horse riding country around The Dover.

Go through the gate here, and almost immediately follow the surfaced lane L, heading south-west. When after 350 yards this turns sharp right, go straight on along a grassy, sometimes boggy, bridleway heading west. In another 400 yards a bridleway joins from the R. Do <u>not</u> go left, but find a wide, possibly unsignposted, path opposite that goes almost parallel through the woods.

MAP FOR WALK 2
(OS Pathfinder map 1306)

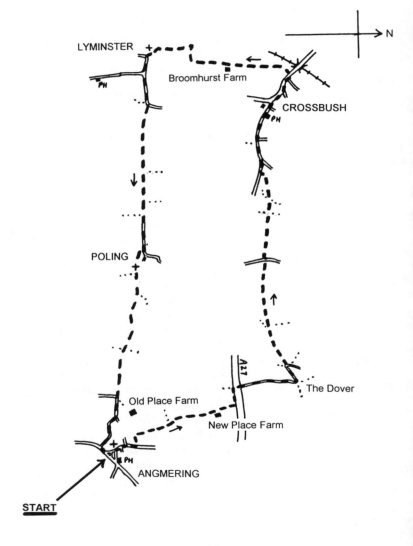

Now continue to walk west. If mud makes parts of the path too sticky you can usually avoid it by diverting into the woods on either side - but make sure that you don't lose sight of the correct path. Half a mile after the bridleway cross a lane and continue west along a public footpath through the next section of woods. Go straight on at a crosspaths, and in a further 100 yards where a bridleway joins from the R, again take a path opposite - not the main one that goes to its L.

Emerging from the woods near a cottage L, go straight on for another 100 yards along a narrow path between hedgerows. This ends at Woodbridge House, dating from 1787. Turn L to the road and then R along a roadside path into CROSSBUSH. It is hard to believe that until 1993 this quiet lane carried the A27 coastal trunk route.

Pass (or stop at) the Plough and Sail pub R and Howards Hotel L. At the road junction turn R along the path beside the main road as it drops to the Arun valley, giving a superb view of Arundel. The Roman Catholic cathedral, parish church and castle (ancestral home of the Dukes of Norfolk) are prominent.

Just after passing the lane to Warningcamp cross the main road and take a footpath that leads down some steps and south-west across a field to a stile. Now there is a short climb to another stile before the direction changes to south. As you drop steadily, head for the square tower of Lyminster church, which now appears about a mile away to the south.

Pass Broomhurst Farm L, and when you arrive at a brook in a deep cutting, bear R, noting another good view of Arundel. At a stile across the brook walk south again, cross a wider stream and enter a narrow path between reeds. Go L at the churchyard wall and visit the church of St Mary Magdalene, LYMINSTER.

The church was begun by the Saxons, but most of what survives is 13th century. It has an extraordinarily large nave roof, and the interior is surprisingly long and high. Look out for the impressive model, built by a local parishioner, of Jerusalem as it was in the time of Christ.

Now take the lane leading east, opposite the lych gate. Join the Arundel-Littlehampton road and continue east. When this bears L, leave it for a bridleway, with Old Vicarage Cottage L. Notice as you still go east, the outskirts of Wick, several glasshouses and the long, flat shape of Body Shop headquarters, all R.

After one mile on this bridleway it enters POLING. Walk through the village, past attractive cottages and gardens. Just before a L bend in the road, take a footpath R to visit St Nicholas's church.

The church is small but light and welcoming. It has a Saxon nave and font, a 14th century chancel and a 15th century tower with a pyramidal cap. Look for its ground-level pulpit and its souvenirs of RAF connections in the Second World War.

Walk east through the churchyard and leave it by a stile in the east wall. Go L and then R to find a footpath heading east, with the green mound of Highdown Hill on the horizon. Go through a large metal gate L and continue east along a track. At another metal gate continue east and cross a field, making for the south-east corner. Cross the footbridge over Black Ditch to some steps leading to another stile. Your way has been fairly straight since leaving Lyminster, and it may come as no surprise to learn that a Roman Villa was excavated on this site. There are no traces of it now.

Now cross the large field in the direction of the red roofs of Angmering in the east, crossing further stiles. Enter the village along a lane, with Old Place Farm L. Pass the prosperous houses of the Ham Manor estate. Turn L on reaching the main road and you are back in the centre of ANGMERING.

Walk 3

PATCHING AND CLAPHAM

Patching Pond - Patching - Michelgrove - Myrtle Grove Farm - Clapham - Patching Pond

Patching and Clapham face each other across a shallow valley, as do the downland settlements of Michelgrove and Myrtle Grove. This is an easy ramble visiting all four. There are a few muddy sections, but most of the walking is on surfaced lanes or hard tracks. Pub/restaurant at start and finish point.

Distance 5½ miles   **Climbing** 400ft   **Highest point** 250ft

Start in the layby at Patching Pond, on the old Worthing-Arundel road east of the Horse and Groom, PATCHING (*map ref TQ 087056*).

Walk west past the Horse and Groom, and turn first R up France Lane. Continue north as the lane becomes the main street through Patching village. Fork L in front of a privet hedge to visit the parish church of St John the Divine.
Patching church dates almost entirely from the 13th century, the exceptions being the rather top-heavy shingled spire and the vestry, which were added at the time of a sub-stantial restoration in the 19th century. The interior is dark, as nearly all of the windows have stained glass, but there are some fine arches and a 15th century octagonal font.
Leave by the brick lych gate, walk down the drive for about 40 yards and then turn R to walk through a farm. Immediately after passing some silos R, turn R to walk north on a broad footpath. At a T-junction turn R again, and walk east, noting good views of Patching church and Highdown Hill behind it.
In 250 yards go through a gate, carry straight on at a crosspaths and walk down hill, passing a reservoir R. Note the twin round towers of a pumping station in the valley ahead. Just before a gate by a clump of trees take a footpath

MAP FOR WALK 3
(OS Pathfinder map 1306)

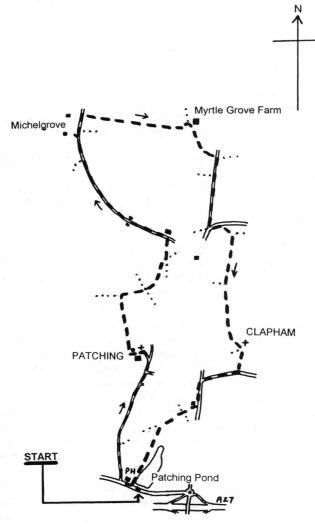

L and walk beside the fence R. Cross a stile and drop down to the riding stables.

Turn L along the tarmac lane and stay on it for nearly a mile as it goes between a pair of lodges that look like book-ends, and past the houses and cottages of the Michelgrove estate L. Just after a high flint and brick wall R, turn R on a bridleway that goes east, into a shallow valley and out the other side into flint built Myrtle Grove Farm. Arriving there, turn L and almost immediately go R between the barns. Now follow the lane through the farm and in 400 yards turn R on a straight track leading south for nearly ½ mile.

Emerge on A280 Long Furlong road, turn L for 10 yards and then cross it to pick up a path carved into the grass bank opposite. In another 200 yards go over a stile and walk south again beside a fence, and later a hedge R. After enter-ing a second field the path veers L, goes up to a kissing gate and enters a wood called Church Copse. Continue in the same direction through the wood for 400 yards until you emerge in a clearing outside the parish church of CLAPHAM.

The church of St Mary the Virgin dates originally from Norman times, but most of its flint fabric is 13th century Early English with some Perpendicular windows. Inside there are some interesting monuments and brasses.

Leave by the lych gate and turn L. Walk down the lane to Clapham's village street, go R along it and once more meet A280. Turn L on the roadside path for 250 yards, and leave it at the village hall R. Take the footpath going south-west across the field, carry straight on at a crosspaths, and after crossing a stile at the bottom of the valley bear L towards another stile in a hedge. Do not cross it, but turn L to walk south, keeping the hedge R as Patching Pond reappears L. Keep going south to arrive back at the Horse and Groom.

MAP FOR WALKS 4 AND 5
(OS Pathfinder map 1306)

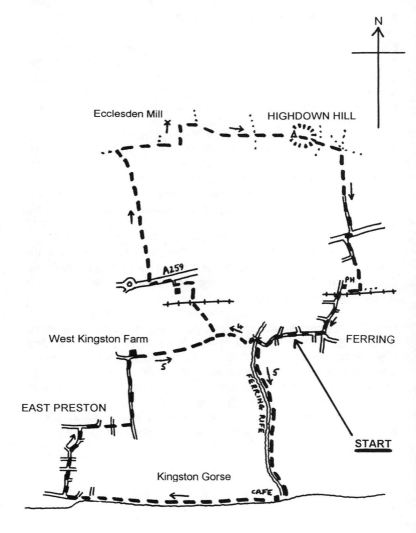

N

Ecclesden Mill

HIGHDOWN HILL

A259

West Kingston Farm

FERRING

EAST PRESTON

START

Kingston Gorse

PH

FERRING RIFE

CAFE

Walk 4

HIGHDOWN

Ferring - Ferring Rife - Ecclesden - Highdown Hill - Ferring

A very easy walk that requires very little effort but offers a splendid all round view from Highdown, an isolated down north of Ferring. There's a pub near the finish. The walk may be combined with Walk 5, which includes a visit to the sea.

Distance 4 miles   **Climbing** 250ft   **Highest point** 266ft

Start in Rife Way, FERRING, near the green opposite the shops (*map ref TQ 094028*).

Walk west along Rife Way and go through the gate at the end. Turn L on a tarmac lane and stay on it as it turns west. Cross a bridge over the Ferring Rife, and at once turn L along its bank. In 20 yards go over a stile R to take a path heading west beside a brook L. About 300 yards from the Rife fork R on a footpath that crosses the field diagonally towards some large barns.

Cross the railway with great care and go due north, passing some red brick houses L. Then turn L to join a concrete lane for 100 yards before you arrive on the A259 dual carriageway. Turn L and walk along the cycle path. When you are halfway to the roundabout cross the road, find a track leading north and walk up it for just over ½ mile. Then pass a gate and turn R along a bridleway that rises gently through an avenue of young trees.

Pass the Ecclesden windmill L, a four-storey black tower mill that is now capless and converted to residential use, and 100 yards further on take a path L between fields. Climb gently, and when the mill is on your L, turn R along the top of the ridge to reach the summit of HIGHDOWN HILL in just over ½ mile.

Highdown has a long history. There was a settlement here in the late Bronze Age (1000BC). A hillfort was con-

structed on it in the Iron Age (around 600BC), and around 450AD it was used as a cemetery by the Anglo Saxons. Now it is owned by the National Trust.

From the trig point on the ramparts there is a view west, along the coast past Littlehampton and Bognor to Chichester Cathedral and the Isle of Wight, and to the masts on the downs at Bignor Hill. To the north are the villages of Patching and Clapham. Walk a few yards east and you will see the coast from Worthing to Brighton and the cliffs beyond, while Cissbury Ring looms to the north-east.

Keep going east, and look out for the top of a reservoir R. Now turn south, pass the reservoir R and continue south along the L side of a large field. Pass through the nurseries and emerge once more on the A259.

Cross the road and go down Ferring Lane. When this bends R take a footpath L to head south across a field. Then turn R along the north side of the railway line until you come to a level crossing opposite the Henty Arms, FERRING. Now cross the railway and take the second turning R (Rife Way), to get back to your starting point.

The converted mill at Ecclesden *(Walk 4)*

24

Walk 5

FORGOTTEN RIVER

Ferring - Ferring Rife - Kingston Gorse - East Preston - West
Kingston - Ferring

*The Ferring Rife, only two miles long, is the forgotten river of Sussex. This walk
enjoys the peace and beauty of its banks, and one of the few remaining unspoiled sections of coastline in West Sussex. Refreshments and toilets at the Lemon
Tree Cafe. The walk may be combined with Walk 4, which has a bit of climbing.*

Distance 4 miles   **Climbing** 20ft   **Highest Point** 20ft

Start in Rife Way, FERRING, near the green opposite the
shops (*map ref TQ 094028*).

Walk west along Rife Way and go through the gate at
the end. Turn L on a tarmac lane and stay on it as it turns
west. Do not cross the bridge, but turn L to walk along the
east bank of the Ferring Rife, all the way to its end at the car
park of the Lemon Tree cafe. The Rife runs under the shingle
here, and flows into the sea on the shingle shore.

Now go through a kissing gate west of the cafe, and
walk west for one mile on the greensward between the sea
and the private estates of Kingston Gorse and West Kingston.
When the grass ends continue to go west along a path behind
beach huts, and then along a road. You are now in the parish
of EAST PRESTON. Take the second turning R, which
leaves at a planted triangle with a post box in its middle.
Walk north for 600 yards and turn R into Vermont Drive.

When this road ends go straight on along a path,
cross a road and continue along the path opposite. When you
meet a lane turn L along it for ¼ mile until it bends sharply L.
Here turn R on a footpath through West Kingston Farm and
head east across stiles and fields for nearly a mile until you
are back at the bridge over Ferring Rife. Cross it, and follow
the lane back to Rife Way, FERRING, where you started.

MAP FOR WALKS 6 AND 7
(OS Pathfinder map 1287)

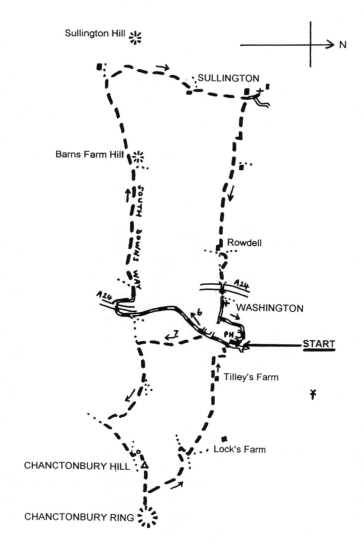

26

Walk 6

SULLINGTON

Washington - Highden Hill - Barns Farm Hill - Sullington Hill - Sullington - Rowdell - Washington.

A fine two-mile stretch of the South Downs Way is followed by a superb bostal path descending the downs, and visits to two contrasting parish churches. The second half can be a bit sticky after heavy rain. This walk can be combined with Walk 7 to provide a nine-mile ramble with a visit to the Frankland Arms (and your car) at half way.

Distance 5½ miles   **Climbing** 550ft   **Highest point** 675ft

Start on the old Worthing road, opposite the Frankland Arms, WASHINGTON (*map ref TQ 122129*).

Walk south along the road for just over ½ mile until it meets the A24 trunk road. Now follow the South Downs Way signs to cross this busy highway and walk up Glaseby Lane opposite. After a steep climb at first, pass through a metal gate and continue on the South Downs Way as it becomes a hard track on fairly level ground over Highden Hill and Barns Farm Hill. There are good views back to Chanctonbury and Cissbury Rings.

Keep on the South Downs Way until you reach an iron gate R, about 100 yards before a large Dutch barn L. Go through the gate to take a bostal path that describes a semicircle around a deep coombe just below the summit of Sullington Hill. As it veers north this bridleway drops more steeply before passing Hill Barn R and becoming a concrete track leading into the hamlet of SULLINGTON. Notice a fine view of Kithurst Hill L.

Sullington's parish church of St Mary is a squat building with a dark interior. It has Saxon and Norman work in the nave and tower walls, but most of what you see now is Early English. The church was damaged in the hurricane of 1987

but has been well repaired. Inside there is a 13th century, life-size effigy of a knight in chain mail, lying on a Saxon stone coffin. Look out for the adjoining Manor Farmhouse and an unusual war memorial - a lamp column formed by an ancient mill-roller.

Leaving the lychgate, go back 50 yards to a barn in the farmyard R, pass it and take a bridleway L going east, keeping a hedge on your L. The conical shape of Sullington Hill is on the southern horizon, and Barns Farm Hill is on your R. Keep walking east, past Barns Farm and Home Farm Cottages, Rowdell. After being diverted L and then R, the bridleway takes on a tarmac surface, crosses a bridge over A24 and passes the parish church of WASHINGTON.

Also dedicated to St Mary, this sandstone church was almost completely rebuilt in 1867, but the tower dates from the 15th century. The interior is spacious but dark, having small and heavily stained glass windows.

About 100 yards after the church, turn L down School Lane, pass the school and some playing fields, and emerge at the Frankland Arms for some welcome refreshment.

The parish church of St Mary, Sullington *(Walk 6)*

Walk 7

CHANCTONBURY THE SHORT WAY

Washington - Washington Bostal - Chanctonbury dewpond - Chanctonbury Hill - Chanctonbury Ring - Tilley's Farm - Washington.

Washington nestles at the foot of one of Sussex's favourite hills, Chanctonbury. The famous clump of beeches planted in 1760 by Charles Goring of Wiston was decimated by severe gales in 1987 and 1990, but the hill is still worth a visit for its Iron Age hillfort the 'Ring', a well-restored dewpond and extensive views on all sides. The paths are steep in places, and can be muddy after wet weather. This walk can be combined with Walk 6 to provide a nine-mile ramble with a visit to the Frankland Arms (and your car) at half way.

Distance 3½ miles   **Climbing** 625ft   **Highest point** 783ft

Start on the old Worthing road, opposite the Frankland Arms, WASHINGTON (*map ref TQ 122129*).

Walk south along the road for ¼ mile, and then find a footpath L, opposite Stocks Mead. Cross two stiles and head across the meadow towards the middle of a wood. Go over another stile and continue through the trees by the obvious path. After a short but steep climb the path levels out by a quarry R. A few yards further on it joins the South Downs Way.

Turn L and L again for the steady plod up the Washington Bostal track. After just over ½ mile this arrives on the downland ridge, where it is joined by the bridleway from Findon. Turn L and walk towards the remains of the wind-damaged tree clump on the summit of Chanctonbury. Where another bridleway joins from the L, cross a stile L to visit the beautiful dewpond, restored by the Society of Sussex Downsmen in 1970 and kept in good order ever since. Go over the stile on the east side of the pond, and walk to the trig point on CHANCTONBURY HILL for a splendid view.

To the east is Chanctonbury Ring, while to the south-east you may spot the skyscrapers of Brighton and the cliffs beyond.   Cissbury Ring is the long hill due south, with Worthing to its R. In the south-west the coastline extends past Littlehampton and Bognor Regis, and on a very clear day you might see the silhouette of the Isle of Wight on the horizon. Westward the Sussex downs stretch away past Kithurst Hill to their highest point, Tegleaze, while to the north lies the vast area of woods and fields known as the Weald.   Beyond this you might see the distant sandy ridges around Blackdown and Leith Hill and the chalk quarries of the North Downs, while in the foregound stands the sail-less smock mill at Rock, just above the sand quarries, with the village of Ashington just beyond.

Now walk on springy turf to CHANCTONBURY RING, an Iron Age enclosure of 3½ acres, enclosed by a circular rampart.   Within this Charles Goring planted his famous beeches more than 200 years ago, and we can only hope that the replacement saplings planted in recent years will one day provide the same delight.

From the Ring, go back towards the trig point, and find a small gate R beyond which is a bridleway that descends the hillside in a north-westerly direction.   When it enters the woods, keep going north-west, at first steeply, and then on more level ground as other bridleways join from the R.

Reaching a large field opposite Locks Farm and Rock Mill, turn R on a footpath along the edge of the wood.   In just over 100 yards take the bridleway L to a crosspaths at the corner of the large field L.   Take the L footpath, and cross the field diagonally.   Cross a second field as far as the end of a hedge.   Now walk due west with the hedge on your R.   Pass Tilley's Farm, and then go over a stile R to take a footpath across a meadow with a tile-hung house L.

Now the Frankland Arms at WASHINGTON comes into sight. Follow the footpath signs across a second meadow and a private drive. Keep going between fences, pass over a footbridge and emerge on the road, back at the Frankland Arms.

Walk 8

FINDON

High Salvington - West Hill - Church Hill - Findon - Roger's Farm - High Salvington.

A short and easy ramble over the downs to the attractive village of Findon, which has pubs, restaurants and small shops. The return walk passes the restored windmill at High Salvington.

Distance 5 miles **Climbing** 330ft **Highest point** 457ft

Start at the small car park at the north end of West Hill, HIGH SALVINGTON, where the surfaced road turns into a rough bridleway (*map ref TQ 122069*).

Walk north-west along the bridleway, and notice almost immediately the views L to Littlehampton, Bognor Regis, the spire of Chichester cathedral and the Isle of Wight downs; and R to Cissbury Ring across the valley.

Pass the mast R and continue along the top of the long ridge of West Hill. Stay on the same track for 1½ miles with a fine view L to Blackpatch Hill and Tolmare Farm, and eventually arrive on the A280 Long Furlong road.

Walk R along the grass verge for 10 yards and then go R up to and over a stile. Head south-east on a footpath across a field for 50 yards, and then go down to another stile. Cross it and continue south-east down hill towards Cissbury and Findon. This path will bring you to the parish church of FINDON.

The church of St John the Baptist, dating from the 11th century, is built entirely of flint. It has a 13th century tower with a shingled broach spire and, although the interior was heavily restored in 1867 there are interesting features, including a 13th century screen.

Now go east down the lane in front of the lych gate past 18th century Findon Place R. Cross the A24 Worthing-

MAP FOR WALK 8
(OS Pathfinder map 1306)

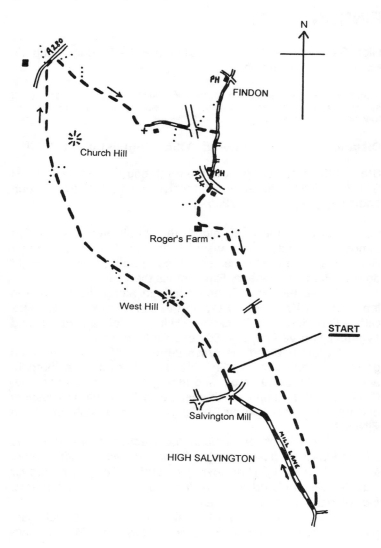

N

A280

FINDON

PH

Church Hill

A24

PH

Roger's Farm

West Hill

START

Salvington Mill

HIGH SALVINGTON

MILL LANE

London road and continue down the footpath opposite into the village. Turn L for the Gun Inn, restaurants and shops, and R for a cafe and the Black Horse pub.

Leave the village by walking south down the main street. Cross the A24 dual carriageway opposite the Black Horse, turn L for 20 yards, and before the garden centre turn R up Roger's Lane. In less than ½ mile, go L in front of the white farmhouse of Roger's Farm and in 10 yards follow the bridleway heading east up a gentle gradient in the direction of Cissbury.

Soon the bridleway veers south. After a further ¼ mile cross a lane and continue to walk south, firstly along 'The Gallops' at the L side of a recreation ground and then along a bridleway between bushes.

When the bridleway ends at an unmade road (Mill Lane) turn sharp R to walk along it north-west and uphill for more than ½ mile past some desirable homes. At the junction with Furze Road is the windmill at HIGH SALVINGTON.

This is one of only two post mills surviving in West Sussex. It was built in the 18th century in a superb position on open downland 350 feet above sea level. The mill stopped grinding corn in 1897, but in the 1930s was open to the public with teas being served in the roundhouse at its base. It is now owned by Worthing Borough Council and has been well restored, thanks to the efforts of the Friends of High Salvington Mill.

Now cross the road and walk up West Hill, back to the car park where you started.

MAP FOR WALK 9
(OS Pathfinder maps 1287 and 1306)

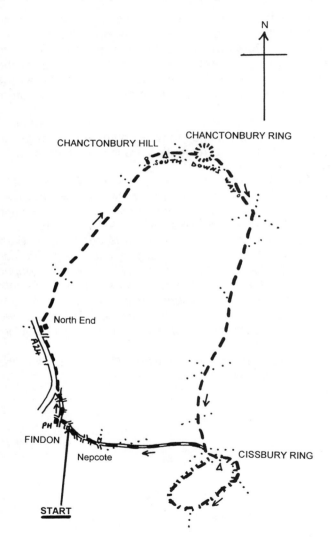

Walk 9

TWO RINGS

Findon - North End - Chanctonbury Ring - Cissbury Ring - Nepcote Green - Findon

The great hillforts, Chanctonbury Ring and Cissbury Ring, are two of the most familiar landmarks in Sussex. Here they are combined in a splendid ramble on gentle gradients and firm ground. Pubs and cafes at Findon only.

Distance 7½ miles   **Climbing** 900ft   **Highest point** 783ft

Start at the layby alongside the little green in Nepcote Lane, FINDON, about 50 yards from the Gun Inn (*map ref TQ 123088*).

Walk down Nepcote Lane to the Gun Inn and turn R along the village street. When this joins the Worthing-London trunk road continue northward, on the surfaced footpath running parallel with, but well set back from, the road. In less than ½ mile, just after crossing the lane R to Findon Park House, take a track R at North End and begin a gradual ascent between the hedgerows.

Within another ½ mile the damaged clump of beeches on the summit of Chanctonbury comes into view in the northeast. Continue along the same path, and in another mile join the South Downs Way, which comes in L after its ascent from Washington. Near the top of the climb look for a stile L. Go over it to visit the Chanctonbury dewpond. Then go over another stile and make for the concrete trig point on CHANCTONBURY HILL between the dewpond and the Ring. *The view from here is described in Walk 7.*

Now make for the Iron Age hillfort that is CHANCTONBURY RING.

Here in 1760 Charles Goring of Wiston planted the beeches that were a much-loved Sussex landmark until they were blown down by the 'hurricane' of 1987 and a further gale

in 1990. A few younger trees outside the ramparts were spared, and saplings have now been planted inside the Ring to restore its status as a landmark.

Now walk east, away from the Ring, enjoying the view of the downs from Truleigh to Wolstonbury, with Steyning, Bramber and Beeding below them and Wiston at your feet. Pass another dewpond R, next to an iron water tank, and in ½ mile take the bridleway R, leading south towards Cissbury Ring. Go straight on for two miles, ignoring all paths to L and R until you reach the small car park at the foot of the Ring.

Start up the hillside, but after 100 yards bear L and ascend the hill by the spiral path that takes you round its east side. Near the top go through a small, wooden gate and turn R to get to the massive ramparts of CISSBURY RING.

The Ring, owned by the National Trust, is a huge Iron Age fort with a double rampart, the inner of which is over a mile round and encloses 65 acres. In the Stone Age it was a flint-mining centre with about 250 pits, some of which were 40 feet deep. The ramparts and ditches of the hillfort were begun around 3000 BC, to protect the settlers within.

The walk along the ramparts rivals that on the town walls of any medieval city. Start southward by climbing the steps on the rampart, and notice the domed shape of Steep Down in the east. As you walk on, most of Worthing comes into view, beyond the Hill Barn golf course. Rounding the south-west corner the modern development in the Findon Valley dominates the foreground, with Salvington windmill just beyond. Don't forget to look R to see the grass-covered spoil heaps and hollows left by the Stone Age flint miners. Along the western rampart you can see Findon village and church, and soon Chanctonbury appears on the northern horizon. When the Cissbury car park is immediately below, drop down from the rampart, cross a stile and descend to the car park.

Now take the surfaced lane L, going steadily down towards Findon. At the first road junction ignore a turn L and continue down Nepcote Lane past the large green L. Bear R at the shops, and very soon you will be back at your starting point, close to the pubs and cafes of FINDON.

Walk 10

CISSBURY

Broadwater - Mount Carvey - Cissbury Ring - Tenants Hill - Broadwater

The downs are rich in prehistoric hillforts, constructed in an age when all human settlements were on the summits of hills, and needed protection from the dangers of the Wealden forests and foreign invaders. One of the largest of these is Cissbury Ring, now a National Trust property. Originally a primitive factory where flints were mined and shaped, it was fortified in the Iron Age by a double rampart and ditch, enclosing about 60 acres. This walk on a gentle gradient visits the summit of Cissbury for its fine view, but if there is time you should also walk around the high inner rampart. No refreshments on this walk.

Distance 4½ miles   **Climbing** 530ft   **Highest point** 602ft

Start in the small car park at the entrance to the recreation ground in Hill Barn Lane, about 100 yards north of the BROADWATER roundabout (*map ref TQ 142051*).

Turn L out of the car park, walk south to the round-about and then R on the path beside Warren Road. After No. 100 turn R along an unmade road that quickly becomes a bridleway climbing steadily past, and later through, the Hill Barn golf course. Keep going north for nearly 1½ miles, ignoring all paths to L and R. Near the top, go through a gate across the way and pause to look at the westward view, which embraces the built up areas of Worthing and Findon Valley with a backcloth of Highdown Hill, West Hill, Salvington (with the mast) and Church Hill, sheltering Findon's ancient church. Continue north into the small wood that guards the southern boundary of CISSBURY RING and emerge on the ramparts. Walk up the chalk path between them, and then straight across the centre of the hillfort, making for the highest ground on which stands the trig point at 602 feet. Stop to take in a superb all-round view.

MAP FOR WALK 10
(OS Pathfinder map 1306)

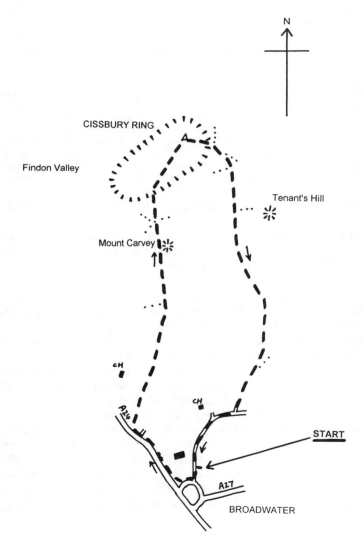

Chanctonbury stands on the northern horizon, while to its R is the long, high ridge carrying the South Downs Way. To the east you may see a short piece of Weald, and then the high downs of Newtimber Hill, Dyke Hill and Truleigh Hill. In the south the coastal plain stretches beyond the tower blocks of Brighton in the east and to Littlehampton in the west. The west view is of the downs beyond Findon, including Blackpatch, Kithurst and Barnsfarm Hills.

Make for the gap in the high ramparts to the east. Pass through it, and beyond a gate take a chalky bridleway that heads south, with the valley and its golf course now R. After just over 1½ miles pass a large flint barn L and continue down the track. At a T-junction turn R along the road, pass the golf club R and soon afterwards arrive back at your starting point north of BROADWATER.

Downland flora:
Salad Burnet, Round-headed Rampion, Horseshoe Vetch
Stemless Thistle

MAP FOR WALK 11
(OS Pathfinder map 1306)

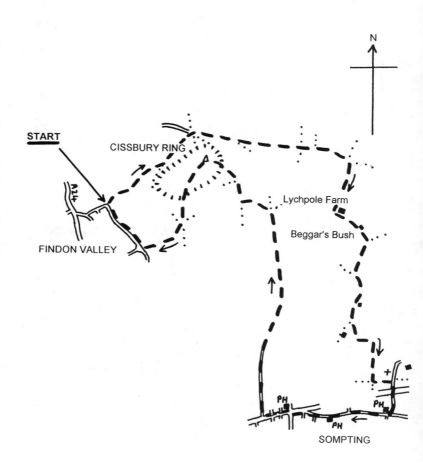

Walk 11

THE RHENISH HELM

Findon Valley - Lychpole Farm - Beggars Bush - Sompting -
Tenants Hill - Cissbury Ring - Findon Valley

*A ramble on easy gradients. The highlights are Sompting's Saxon church with
its unique tower (the `Rhenish Helm') and the magnificent hillfort of Cissbury
Ring, which is in view for most of the way. Pubs in Sompting village.*

Distance 9½ miles   **Climbing** 1020ft   **Highest point** 602ft

Start at the Cissbury Ring car park at the east end of Storrington Rise, FINDON VALLEY, where it meets Long Meadow
(map ref TQ 128077). The car park is signposted 'Cissbury
Ring' from the A24, and accessed from May Tree Avenue.

Leave the car park at its north-east corner, along a
gently climbing bridleway that skirts the steep slopes of Cissbury R. Keep going for about a mile until you arrive at
another car park, right under the north face of the hill. Save
the summit for your return journey, and take a chalky track
leading east and down hill from the car park. As you go, the
prominent round hill ahead is Steep Down.
Stay on this track for just over a mile, until immediately after a small rise where the path divides to go either side
of a small clump of trees. At the top turn R at a crosspaths,
and now walk south to Lychpole Farm in the valley. Pass the
farmhouse of boulder flints L and continue down a concrete
track to the barns at Beggars Bush.
When the concrete lane turns L, go R to pass two
more barns R, and head south on a bridleway below Cissbury's eastern slopes. In 400 yards pass through a gate and
continue south. The path goes round the side of a hill and
past the ruins of Coombe Barn L. Continue along a flinty track
that wends its way up the side of the hill.

Just below the top take a footpath L that heads south along a grass terrace. Go through a small gate and continue south beside a large field L. When you arrive at a panoramic view of Lancing, Sompting and Worthing follow the path L, and in 200 yards go R and walk south, straight down the hill. This gives a good view L of the tall, slender tower of Sompting's ancient parish church, and the adjoining chapel ruins and modern parish buildings to the north. At the next crosspaths turn L along a path that gives access to the churchyard. Now it is time to visit the beautiful church of St Mary the Virgin, SOMPTING.

The distinctive, gabled, helmet-like top of the tower is a style unique in England but not along the Rhine, and therefore is known as a 'Rhenish Helm' . The interior of the church is light, spacious and a haven of peace and tranquillity. Although the building is cruciform (cross-shaped), it is smaller than you might expect. There is a remarkably fine Saxon arch where the nave joins the tower, and many examples of Norman architecture and the church's historical connections with the Knights Templar and the Order of the Hospital of St John of Jerusalem.

Leaving St Mary's, walk south down the lane, cross the A27 dual carriageway and continue down Church Lane to the Marquis of Granby pub. Turn R to head west for more than ½ mile along Sompting's village street, past the Gardener's Arms L and Upton Farm House R, before it filters into the A27 trunk road.

Continue to go west along the roadside path, cross the main road opposite The Downlands restaurant, and go west again. Pass Pines Avenue and Beeches Avenue, and then go R on a public bridleway between the houses. This becomes a track lined with trees and bushes, as it slowly climbs past the Hill Barn golf course towards the top of Tenants Hill.

About 1½ miles along this bridleway the bushes end, and there is a view R to Truleigh Hill (with the masts) and the disused chalk quarry north of Shoreham. Now take a track L that goes west, uphill for a few yards, and then skirts the north end of a deep valley, with good views south to the coast at Worthing.

Arriving on a south-north bridleway turn R and make for the east ramparts of CISSBURY RING, a great Iron Age hillfort owned by the National Trust. Enter the gap in the ramparts and walk west to the trig point on the summit, at 602 feet. *The view is described in Walk 10.*

Now turn to the south and walk towards the trees just beyond the ramparts. Go through the south gap in the ramparts, pass the trees L and fork R along a footpath between fences that at first begins to descend the hillside in the direction of Worthing. After 250 yards take a right turn to drop down more steeply beside a fence R, towards the Findon Valley estate.

Pass a beech hanger L, and emerge on a concrete road called Shepherd's Mead. Turn R and continue as the road becomes Long Meadow and takes you back to the car park in FINDON VALLEY.

Sompting and the coast from the downs *(Walk 11)*

43

MAP FOR WALK 12
(OS Pathfinder map 1287)

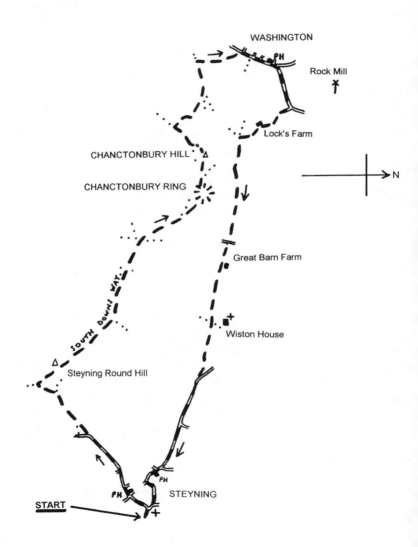

WASHINGTON

Rock Mill

PH

Lock's Farm

CHANCTONBURY HILL

CHANCTONBURY RING

→N

Great Barn Farm

SOUTH DOWNS WAY

Wiston House

Steyning Round Hill

PH

PH

STEYNING

START

44

Walk 12

SOUTH DOWNS WAY & CHANCTONBURY

Steyning - Round Hill - Chanctonbury Ring - Chanctonbury Hill
- Washington - Lock's Farm - Wiston - Steyning

*A splendid section of the South Downs Way to one of the best known landmarks
in Sussex, followed by an easy ramble along the foot of the downs. Best done in
dry or frosty weather, as the return section can be muddy through the woods.
Pub at half way.*

Distance 10 miles   **Climbing** 730ft   **Highest point** 783ft

Start in the large car park off Church Street, STEYNING,
opposite the parish church (*map ref TQ 179113*).

Turn L out of the car park, in front of the church, and
walk along Church Street to its junction with High Street.
Cross the road and walk up Sheep Pen Lane into Newham
Lane. After ½ mile, just past The White House L, go straight
on up a bridleway that ascends steeply. Pause to look back at
the view to Steyning, the flood plains of the Adur and the
downs as far as Wolstonbury in the east.

Continue up the hill to a point where the path levels
out by a seat, and take a bridleway L that goes up hill for a
further 80 yards and then descends for slightly more.   Just
before the bushes turn R, and then R again when you join the
broad track of the South Downs Way.   Now follow the Way
north-west on almost level ground for two miles before the
final short climb to the trees in the hillfort of CHANCTON-
BURY RING - *description in Walk 9.*

Pass the trees R and make for the trig point on
CHANCTONBURY HILL at 783ft. *The view from here is
described in Walk 7.*

Now head west, cross a stile and arrive at the beautiful dewpond, restored in 1970 by the Society of Sussex
Downsmen.   Go over the stile to the south and turn R to

45

resume your walk along the South Downs Way. In ¼ mile follow the Way R and descend the hill by the Washington Bostal path. When this levels out pass a sewage works R and in a further 300 yards leave the South Downs Way by turning R along a footpath.

This passes a quarry L and then drops muddily through a small wood to cross a stile and enter a field. Cross the field diagonally L, and after two more stiles emerge on the former Worthing road. Turn R to reach the Frankland Arms, WASHINGTON - a pub that is proud of its welcome to walkers!

Continuing north, take the road R after the pub, and walk along the verge beside A283 for just over ¼ mile. Now turn R along a concrete track to Lock's Farm. Pass the farm R and continue to the bottom of the hill, where you turn L and walk east along a bridleway into the woods that cloak the north slopes of Chanctonbury.

This sometimes muddy path is never far from the edge of the woods as it first climbs steadily, then drops to a corrugated barn L Eventually it leaves the wood and becomes less muddy. Turn R just after Malt House R and almost immediately go L to continue east. Walk through Great Barn Farm, which has a granary L on staddle stones, and soon afterwards continue along the now tarmac track that passes under a footbridge.

Just after Wiston House and church come into view L take a footpath R along the edge of a large field. Cross a stile and go north for 30 yards, keeping a fence R. Then go L to find another stile. After passing through a small wood follow the footpath signs as they lead you over a footbridge and along the edge of another field before emerging on the lane that will take you all the way back to STEYNING.

Arriving in High Street, turn L to walk down Tanyard Lane and cross Church Lane to visit St Andrew's church before returning to the car park. *The church and town of Steyning are described in Walk 13.*

Walk 13

HORSESHOE AND BOWL

Steyning - Horseshoe (north) - Round Hill - Soper's Bottom - Upper Maudlin Farm - Maudlin - Steyning

A short ramble on clear and mainly firm paths, with good views of Downs, Weald and Adur Valley. There is one long climb early on. Pubs, cafes and toilets in Steyning.

Distance 5 miles   **Climbing** 575ft   **Highest point** 595ft

Start in the large car park off Church Street, STEYNING, opposite the parish church *(map ref TQ 179113).*

       Turn L in front of the church, and immediately go R into Church Lane. Take the next L into Tanyard Lane and walk on to its junction with the High Street. Cross this, and walk up the twitten opposite. At the next road turn R and follow this as it bends towards the downs. About 80 yards after the bend find a footpath L passing the bowling green L.
       Now climb steadily up the northern arm of the Steyning Horseshoe, pausing occasionally to take in the widening view back to Steyning and the downs around Truleigh Hill. Near the top of the hill your path is joined by a bridleway from the R, and soon afterwards it bears L to pass through some young trees on the lip of a deep, wooded coombe L. This is the summit of the Horseshoe, just below the top of STEYNING ROUND HILL.
       Keep on the path going south until you emerge from the trees and the path begins to descend the southern arm of the Horseshoe. At this point take the bridleway going uphill R. On the crest of this hill a fine views unfolds.
       To the north-west is the trig point on Steyning Round Hill, with Chanctonbury beyond. In the east is the downland block around Truleigh and Dyke Hills, with Upper Beeding in the foreground. South-east you might catch a glimpse of the

MAP FOR WALK 13
(OS Pathfinder maps 1287 and 1306)

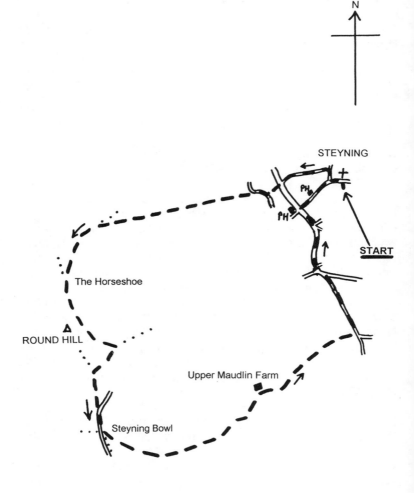

sea at Shoreham and the tower blocks of Brighton, while to the south is dome-like Steep Down, and to its R Worthing and Cissbury Ring.

Join the South Downs Way heading south, and follow it to the Sompting-Steyning road. Walk along the roadside path for about 100 yards. Immediately after the grass car park L, take the concrete bridleway L, descending into Soper's Bottom, renamed Steyning Bowl by the hang gliding and paragliding enthusiasts who take advantage of the 'thermals' here.

Stay on the track all the way down into this beautiful valley. Walk through Upper Maudlin Farm, and then past prosperous-looking modern homes with landscaped gardens. At a T junction about 1½ miles from the top, turn L along the path above the road, and 50 yards on continue on the path on the R side of the road. At the next T-junction go L and follow the road back into STEYNING.

Steyning is well worth exploring. The sturdy Norman church of St Andrew is built on the site of an eight century church founded by a local saint called Cuthman. The exterior is remarkable for the chequered pattern on the tower, while inside are some splendid ornamental arches and mouldings. The little town is full of delightful buildings of the 15th-19th centuries, including the old Market House, the grammar school, a former gaol, a timber-framed workhouse building, four pubs and several restaurants.

Go down Church Street, past the grammar school, Chantry Green and the parish church, to get back to the car park.

MAP FOR WALK 14
(OS Pathfinder map 1306)

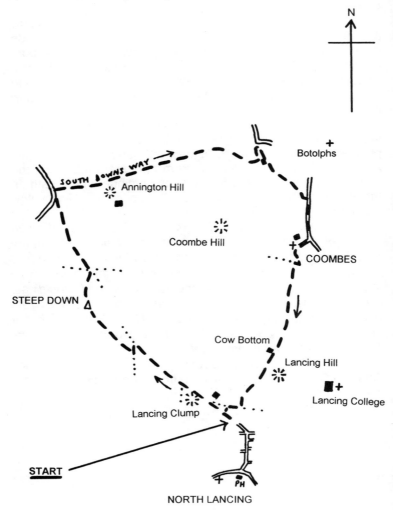

N

SOUTH DOWNS WAY

Botolphs

Annington Hill

Coombe Hill

COOMBES

STEEP DOWN

Cow Bottom

Lancing Hill

Lancing College

Lancing Clump

START

NORTH LANCING

PH

Walk 14

STEEP DOWN AND COOMBES

North Lancing - Lancing Clump - Steep Down - Annington Hill
- Coombes - Cow Bottom - Lancing Hill - North Lancing

*An airy walk over the hills behind Lancing, including the stiff climb of Steep
Down, a panoramic section of the South Downs Way and a visit to the secluded
hamlet and church of Coombes. No refreshments on this route!*

Distance 6½ miles   **Climbing** 700ft   **Highest point** 489ft

Start in the car park at Lancing Ring Nature Reserve, NORTH
LANCING, reached by a lane beyond the northern end of Mill
Road (*map ref TQ 183063*).

Set off northward along the flint bridleway past a disused chalk pit and some derelict farm buildings R, and continue the ascent to pass Lancing Clump L, a distinctive line of
beeches until they were severely damaged by the 'hurricane'
of 1987. Just over the crest of the hill notice the prominent
dome of Steep Down ahead, with Cissbury and Chanctonbury
in attendance behind it on either side.

Keep going on the same track as it heads north-west,
until just before it begins to wind around the north side of the
hill. At the end of the field L, turn L at a signpost and in 20
yards go R up the straight and obvious path that will lead you
to the trig point on the summit of STEEP DOWN at 489ft.

*The view from the top is extensive. On a clear day
you may trace the coastline from Beachy Head in the east to
Littlehampton in the west, with acres of rolling downland on all
sides. In the west, Highdown is the tiny hill nearest the sea,
while north of it stretches the long, high ridge ending at the
Iron Age hillfort of Cissbury Ring. North-west is Chanctonbury, and to its R is Steyning Round Hill. North-east is tree-
topped Coombe Hill, with the village of Upper Beeding and the*

bulky mass of Truleigh Hill beyond. Lancing Clump is south-east, in front of Shoreham and the silvery Adur.

Now follow the same path as it drops north to a tall transmission tower near a crosspaths. Take the bridleway going north up hill with some large barns R. In ½ mile join the Sompting-Steyning road, which fortunately has a grass path on its R side. After about 50 yards take the bridleway R, the South Downs Way, and stay on it as it descends very gradually just L of the top of the broad ridge of Annington Hill, with the deep Maudlin valley L. After nearly a mile on this path you pass L a plantation of conifers and beeches, planted in 1979 to commemorate the diamond jubilee of the Women's Institute. Go through a metal gate just south of the trees and continue to descend at first towards Truleigh Hill and after ¼ mile towards the cement works quarry across the valley.

Where there is a wooden shed near the entrance to Tinpots Cottage follow the track L for 20 yards, and then find a bridleway through the trees R. Go through a wooden gate and turn R, to head south around two sides of a large field. When the path ends go through an iron gate, turn R for 20 yards and then walk up hill through a small wood. On open ground at the top go L for 10 yards and arrive on a road opposite Passie's Pond, a coarse fishing area.

Now turn R and walk along the road for less than ½ mile until you arrive at a telephone kiosk by the lane into COOMBES. Go R, walk the length of the tiny street, and by way of two squeezer stiles enter the church.

Coombes church, which is not dedicated to any saint, is a simple, peaceful downland church with a Norman nave and a chancel only a century younger. Within are some 12th century wall paintings discovered in 1949 and beautifully restored.

Now walk south through the churchyard and go through another squeezer stile into a wood. Follow the path up hill until it emerges on open down. Go R for 10 yards, and then head south over the brow of the hill with a wire fence R. As Lancing College comes into view L, cross a stile and continue south with a fence L. Keep straight on, ignoring tracks to

L and R, and descend to the flint enclosure in the remote valley of Cow Bottom.

Now ascend Lancing Hill by a steep path with a fence L. At the top of this climb, cross a stile L and continue across the broad ridge between Lancing Hill and Lancing Clump. Go straight across the large field that straddles the ridge and after further stiles emerge on a path near the chalk pit you passed at the start. Turn R and pass the chalk pit L to return to the car park in NORTH LANCING.

Coombes church *(Walk 14)*

MAP FOR WALK 15
(OS Pathfinder maps 1287, 1288, 1306 and 1307)

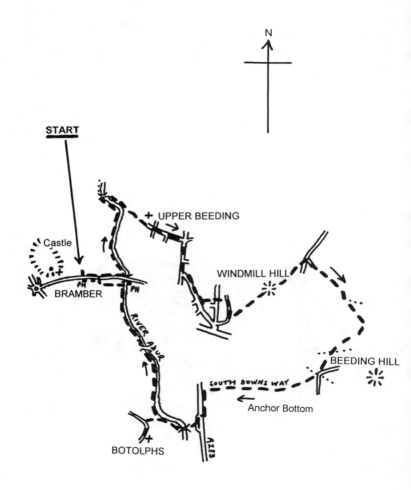

N

START

Castle

+ UPPER BEEDING

WINDMILL HILL

BRAMBER

PH

PH

RIVER ADUR

BEEDING HILL

SOUTH DOWNS WAY

Anchor Bottom

A283

BOTOLPHS

54

Walk 15

BEEDING HILL

Bramber - Upper Beeding - Windmill Hill - Golding Barn - Beeding Hill - Botolphs - Bramber

An easy and delightful walk, visiting two ancient churches and two of the best viewpoints in the Adur valley. Pubs, cafes and toilets in Bramber.

Distance 6 miles   **Climbing** 470ft   **Highest point** 375ft

Start at the car park in the middle of BRAMBER street *(map ref TQ 187107).*

Turn L on leaving the car park. Walk past St Mary's, R, a 15th century timber-framed house built for the monks of Sele Priory, Beeding, wardens of the first Bramber bridge. Just before the present road bridge go down some steps L on to the bank of the Adur. Walk north along the river bank path, enjoying views L to Bramber castle, Steyning Round Hill and Chanctonbury Ring, and R to Truleigh and Beeding Hills.

After ½ mile cross the river by an iron footbridge, turn R and walk back along the eastern bank as far as the next bend. Now turn L to cross a ditch by a wooden footbridge, and ascend a flight of steps to the entrance of UPPER BEEDING church.

A church probably existed here before the Norman Conquest, but it was rebuilt in 1070, and ten years later gained greater importance when it became the priory church of the adjoining Benedictine priory of Sele. There are still traces of Norman architecture, but the church, dedicated to St Peter, was heavily 'restored' by the Victorians.

Walk on down the lane eastward, and then straight on along Deacons Way. At a T-junction turn R into Pound Lane, and after passing the shops of Hyde Square take the next turning L. Just over 200 yards further on go L along a made-up footpath. At its end cross the road, and go R and L into another path. This climbs to reach another road, where you must turn R for 100 yards and then L to leave the built-up area by a footpath that ascends WINDMILL HILL (196 feet).

The windmill has long since vanished, but this little hill is a fine viewpoint because of its isolation from the main block of downs. Notice especially the panorama of green hills lining the western side of the valley - Lancing Clump, Coombe Hill, Steep Down, Annington Hill, Steyning Round Hill and Chanctonbury. To the north there is a good view over the flood plains of the Adur and the Wealden carpet beyond.

Continue over the hill to the Henfield road, go L in front of the petrol station, cross the road at Golding Barn and walk up the surfaced bridleway opposite. After passing a light industrial estate, continue the climb as the bridleway goes past a quarry R. At the end of the quarry fork R to take the lower of two paths. This is a particularly pleasing section, which passes through the deep coombe below Tottington Mount, whose slopes rise L with mountain-like steepness. Then climb steadily to arrive by the six-way sign just below the summit of BEEDING HILL at 375 feet.

The view west is similar to that from Windmill Hill, but now you can see the sea beyond Lancing College and the hillfort at Cissbury, on the horizon behind the hamlet of Botolphs.

Now take the airy path along the ridge on the north side of Anchor Bottom, south-westerly in the direction of dome-shaped Steep Down. The path veers west and drops down to the Shoreham-Steyning road, where you must turn L along the roadside path for about 80 yards. Then cross the road into a lay-by/slip road. Walk L through it for about 50 yards and find a sign indicating that the South Downs Way runs behind the hedge.

Follow the Way, cross the Adur by a bridleway bridge and turn R along the river bank. Notice Botolphs church and hamlet across the field L, in front of two round downs, Coombe Hill and Annington Hill. Just after passing Botolphs, at a bend in the river take the broad track L that leaves the river bank and heads towards Annington Hill. Emerge on a lane and turn L to visit the ancient church at BOTOLPHS.

The inside of the church is beautiful in its sheer simplicity. Dedicated since about 1300 to the seventh century English saint Botolph, it has Saxon work in the nave and chancel walls, and a Saxon chancel arch. Around 1250 the church had to be expanded by building an aisle on the north side of the nave, but this fell into ruin as the village's prosperity declined. There is also a rare Jacobean carved pulpit with sounding board.

Resume the river bank path, and continue for another mile. Just before arriving back at Bramber road bridge, take a footpath L, alongside a hedge. After 200 yards turn R to pass over a footbridge into BRAMBER street, where a L turn will bring you back to the pubs, restaurants and car park.

The Saxon church of St Botolph *(Walk 15)*

MAP FOR WALK 16
(OS Pathfinder maps 1287, 1288, 1306 and 1307)

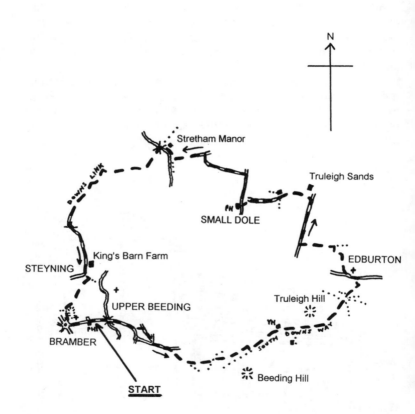

Walk 16

THE DOWNS FROM NEAR AND FAR

Bramber - Upper Beeding - Castle Town - Truleigh Hill - Edburton - Small Dole - Stretham - King's Barn - Bramber

A fine, varied walk that gets to grips with the downs early on, and then descends to the Weald to view them from a distance. It offers a good climb, panoramic views from the South Downs Way, an ancient church, a pub at half way, the river Adur, a disused railway track and the ruins of a Norman castle. Some of the low-lying land on both sides of the Adur is liable to flooding after heavy rain.

Distance 11 miles **Climbing** 750ft **Highest point** 667ft

Start at the car park in the middle of BRAMBER street *(map ref TQ 187107).*

On leaving the car park turn L and walk east along the roadside path of Bramber street. Cross the bridge over the Adur and continue through High Street, UPPER BEEDING. When the road bears R go down the twitten off Hyde Lane straight ahead. Turn R when this meets a road (Hyde Street), in 300 yards join Manor Road, turn R and emerge on A2037 Henfield Road.

Cross the road, turn L and walk on the roadside path for about 300 yards. Then turn R in front of some tile-hung houses, to take a bridleway that soon becomes a steep, stony track. After ¼ mile fork L through a gate, along a bridleway that climbs through some scrub but soon emerges on open downland above an almost sheer drop down to the road you left earlier. The path now climbs less steeply, and offers a good view back to Steyning, Bramber and Beeding, with Chanctonbury Ring on the skyline.

The path ends at a gate on to the bostal path climbing Beeding Hill from Golding Barn. Turn L down this track for 10 yards, and then find a path R that climbs the bank to another gate. Go through it and keep a fence R as you continue on high ground along a terraced path above a deep coombe. When you are almost at the head of the coombe leave this path to climb the bank R to the same fence and cross a stile. Walk across the field to another stile and you are on the South Downs Way. Now stay on the Way for 1¼ miles. Pass the youth hostel and Truleigh Hill masts L and enjoy panoramic views of the Sussex coast R.

When the Way reaches the bottom of a dip, leave it to go a few yards down a bostal track L. You will see R two gravestones erected to the memory of some much-loved pets called Wee Tibby and Wee Tiny (1932) and Dylan (1990). Now turn R up the path that passes north of the memorials. This will bring you back to the South Downs Way, but leave it immediately by going L through a small gate and beginning the descent to Edburton hamlet and church, which from this height look like tiny models at your feet.

Do not take the L turn after 15 yards, but carry on down the terraced path that descends the hillside steeply. At the bottom turn L and in another 100 yards go R to join the road linking the hamlets north of the downs. Now turn L to visit the parish church of EDBURTON.

Dedicated to St Andrew, this sturdy church dates mainly from the 13th century. Simple in stile, its chief treasure is one of the three surviving lead fonts in Sussex. The churchyard is now managed by various conservation bodies as part of the national Living Churchyard scheme.

Continue walking west along the road, cross a stream and take a tarmac lane R. As you walk north, notice the line of downs R, which (from L to R) are Wolstonbury, Newtimber, Dyke, Fulking, Perching and Edburton Hills. After your earlier view of Edburton church from above, you may be surprised to notice that it is built on a small hill. Turn L in front of a tall conifer hedge and in 20 yards go R, keeping a fence R. Do not cross the footbridge at the end of the field, but turn L to head west with a hedge R.

Arriving on a north-south track turn R and head towards the buildings at Truleigh Sands, one of several settlements along a sandy ridge a mile north of the chalk downs. About 150 yards south of the barns go through a gate L and walk around the south and west sides of a small field with a brook L. At the end of the field keep going north on a broad, sandy track. Just over the brow of the hill go through a gate in the hedge L and walk west along the top of a low ridge, with a fence R. You will see Chanctonbury ahead and Henfield on the hill to the north-west. At the end of the field go over a stile and enter Tottington Sands Farm.

Continue to walk west through the farm and out of it along a lane. This gives a fine view of Truleigh Hill in the south. The lane becomes a made up road (Sands Lane). About 200 yards further on take a footpath L that leads down to a footbridge and across a recreation ground to emerge on A2037 opposite the Fox and Hounds pub, SMALL DOLE.

Walk north along the roadside path for about 500 yards. Turn L along New Hall Lane until the way is blocked by a bungalow. Now go R and follow the lane, going first north to a T-junction where you turn L and head west across the meadows, past New Hall Farm L. You are now on the line of a Roman road that crossed Sussex from west to east. The place-names Stretham and Streat (east of Ditchling) are indications of this once important 'street'.

When the surfaced lane bears R to head for Stretham Manor go straight on along a footpath, keeping a hedgerow R. Arriving on the east bank of the Adur (at the point where the Romans forded the river) turn R. Streatham railway bridge lies ahead, and the enlarged and altered medieval manor house is R. Cross a stile at the bridge and you are on the Downs Link path, which here uses the track of the former Shoreham-Horsham railway. Turn L and walk along the track for nearly ½ mile, crossing two streams. Then follow the Downs Link as it leaves the railway track to climb the bank R and head west, up hill between fences.

At a crosspaths at the top turn L down a stony track, passing Wyckham Farm House L, Wyckham Dale Cottages L and Greenfield Farm R before crossing the line of the disused railway by an iron bridge. Keep going along the now tarmac Downs Link past a sewage works and electricity substation R and Kings Barn Farm L into STEYNING.

Where the Downs Link and surfaced road bear R, go over a stile L and head firstly in the direction of an iron bridge and Beeding church beyond it. Stay alongside the fence R as it swings south, and now walk towards Bramber Castle. Cross a stile and continue south above a stream L. When you reach the high bank protecting the castle walls bear R, and when the path bears R beside a half-timbered cottage climb the bank ahead to cross a stile into a grassy area. Walk south through this, and in 100 yards drop down beside a hedge R to join Castle Lane. When this emerges on the Steyning and Bramber bypass at a roundabout turn L and walk up the hill between two turrets to visit the castle and church of BRAMBER.

The village was once an important port and administrative capital of one of the six Rapes of Sussex. The castle was built by William de Braose just after the Norman conquest, but is now only a ruin, owned by the National Trust. The most prominent remains are of a single, 76 foot high, wall of a gatehouse tower, but if you explore the extensive grounds you will find other excavated buildings and most of the castle walls. There is no admission charge.

Just below the castle, on the same hillock, is the Norman church of St Nicholas, once a cruciform building that served as the castle's chapel. There are good views of the Downs from the churchyard.

Walk east down the slope to Bramber street and the car park where you started.

Walk 17

ADUR VALLEY

Shoreham - Shoreham airport - Cuckoo's Corner - Botolphs - Bramber - Old Shoreham - Shoreham.

A straightforward walk on level ground, apart from the short climb to the ruins of Bramber Castle. Transport is never far from the mind on this ramble. Most of it follows the banks of the meandering river Adur, which was once broad and deep enough to carry large ships up to Bramber. It passes through historic Shoreham airport, uses the track of a disused railway that is now a cycle path, crosses a former road toll bridge and goes under two modern, concrete bridges carrying a high volume of road traffic. But you will see also good views of the Downs on either side of the valley and plenty of bird life on the river. There are pubs, cafes and toilets at Bramber.

Distance 10½ miles   **Climbing** 50ft   **Highest point** 50ft

Start in the car park at Adur Recreation Ground, SHOREHAM - just west of the Norfolk Bridge *(map ref TQ 211050).*

Walk north past the toilets L and the Sea Scouts headquarters R, to pass under the iron railway bridge. Now drop down some steps L and turn R to walk along the airport road and do some plane spotting.

It was in July 1910 that a locally built plane made the first flight from this airfield, but the present terminal building dates from only 1936. For most of its life the airport has been used mainly by civil light aircraft, but it has been also the home of aircraft production (Miles and Beagle). It saw active service in both world wars: reminders still exist in the form of brick fortifications at intervals along the river bank.

At the northern end of the airport road turn R, pass the engineering works L, and then immediately take the path L on the western river bank. Follow it as it goes under the concrete road bridge built in 1970 to carry the A27 trunk road north of Shoreham. Notice then the prominent buildings of Lancing College L and the steep slopes of Mill Hill nature reserve R.

MAP FOR WALK 17
(OS Pathfinder maps 1287, 1288, 1306 and 1307)

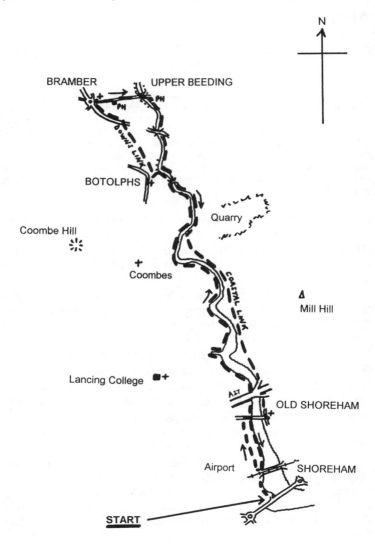

Walk around the creek at Cuckoo's Corner and resume the river bank, with first Applesham Farm and later the hamlet of Coombes on the hills L.

On the east side of the river you can't miss the derelict cement works, with their ugly gash in the chalk hills. After passing the bridge carrying the South Downs Way across the Adur you will see Botolphs church and hamlet across the field L, in front of two round downs, Coombe Hill and Annington Hill. Just after passing Botolphs, at a bend in the river take the broad track L that leaves the river bank and heads towards Annington Hill. Emerge on a lane and turn L to visit the ancient church at BOTOLPHS.

In Roman times the lowest bridge crossing of the Adur was here. A bridge must have existed still in the Middle Ages, when the church was known as St Peter de Vetere Ponte (of the old bridge). Then the Adur almost filled the valley, shipping carried cargoes up to Bramber, and Botolphs was big and important enough to have its own wharf. Now the river is confined to a narrow channel, the shipping and most of the homes have gone, and Botolphs is a sleepy hamlet disturbed only by passing traffic along a minor road. The church is described in Walk 15.

Walk north back along the lane for 150 yards and turn R along the South Downs Way. This time do not go back to the river bank, but turn L on to the Downs Link, along the track of the former Shoreham-Horsham railway that closed in 1966. After ½ mile the main path bears R to head for the river bank. Almost immediately afterwards take the path L, still the Downs Link, and soon emerge on the A283 road.

Cross the road and take up the Downs Link as it goes north west, parallel with the road. When you come to a six-way roundabout, cross The Street, and climb between two flint turrets to visit the castle and church of BRAMBER. *The castle and church are described in Walk 16.*

Go through the lych gate and walk down to the village street. Walk east along it, passing restaurants, cafes, the Castle Inn, the public toilets and half-timbered St Mary's, a 15th century house that is sometimes open to the public.

Cross the river by a narrow road bridge, and take the footpath R, in front of the Bridge public house. Walk along the river bank, passing under the A283 bridge, back to the east side of the South Downs Way bridge you passed earlier.

Now the grassy surface changes to something firmer, for you are now on the Coastal Link cycle path. At first this follows the narrow river bank, but after passing the cement works it turns L to leave the bank and use the track of the old railway, all the way back to Old Shoreham Bridge. Pass under the incredible concrete architecture of the A27 flyover, and on arriving at the wooden trestled bridge, turn L and cross the road to visit the church at OLD SHOREHAM.

Dedicated, like Bramber, to the patron saint of mariners, St Nicolas's was built by the Saxons, but enlarged and beautified by the Normans. Notice the two blocked Saxon doorways in the nave, the magnificent Norman architecture of the tower and transepts, especially the mouldings and carvings of the interior tower arches, and a rare Norman tie-beam at the east end of the nave.

Now go back to Old Shoreham Bridge, and cross it.

Built in 1781 to replace a ferry, and rebuilt in 1916, this bridge carried south coast road traffic over the Adur until 1970, when it was replaced by the flyover to the north. For much of its history it was owned by the railway company, to which motorists and others had to pay a toll at the railway crossing. Since the end of 1970 the bridge has been exclusive to walkers, cyclists, horse riders and anglers. The carriageway was laid with a wooden surface in 1985.

Now take the river bank path, its surface of concrete blocks being another relic of the airport's use during the Second World War. Pass under the iron railway bridge, and then leave the river bank to return to the car park where you started.

Walk 18

A DOMESDAY SETTLEMENT

Mill Hill - Old Erringham - New Erringham - Mill Hill.

A short and easy walk that includes parts of the Mill Hill local nature reserve and passes through Old Erringham Farm, the site of a settlement mentioned in Domesday Book. No refreshment places.

Distance 2½ miles   **Climbing** 250ft   **Highest point** 330ft

Start in the **southern** car park of the Mill Hill nature reserve, OLD SHOREHAM - about 100 yards north of the bridge over A27 *(map ref TQ 212067).* If this is full, there is a larger car park ½ mile up the road, and you can pick up the walk there.

Observe firstly the view south-west to Shoreham airport, Lancing and Worthing and west to Lancing College, Steep Down and the Adur valley. Then take the path going north through the grass, parallel to the road R. After about 300 yards go through a small gate L, just before the large green hump of a downland reservoir. Walk along a footpath that descends to the base of the steep south-west facing slope of MILL HILL.

This is called locally the Butterfly Bank. In times past the grassland here, grazed by sheep and rabbits, was rich in chalk flora, and in summer the hill was alive with thousands of butterflies, including Chalk Hill Blue, Adonis Blue, Clouded Yellow and Fritillaries. Grazing ended and the rabbit population was almost wiped out by myxomatosis in the 1950s, allowing coarse grasses, hawthorn and brambles to take a hold. The hill had begun to revert to its natural state of scrub and woodland. Now, however, the site is being managed as a local nature reserve, and various conservation measures, including winter grazing, are resulting in a return of chalk-loving plants and butterflies.

MAP FOR WALK 18
(OS Pathfinder map 1307)

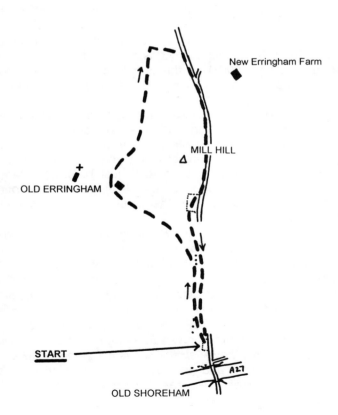

N

New Erringham Farm

MILL HILL

△

+

OLD ERRINGHAM

START

A27

OLD SHOREHAM

The path enters some bushes at the far end of the bank. Continue on it and emerge at a stile leading on to a meadow. Cross the stile and walk towards OLD ERRINGHAM farm in the west. Enter the farm by a large gate. Bear R, passing flint and brick barns R, and then head north up the hill.

Erringham was a settlement mentioned in the Domesday Book of 1086. Although now only a farm, it still possesses two fine medieval houses and a tiny Norman chapel - now used as a barn - which is the only remaining part of a larger church building. This is on the far side of the farm, just R of the three tile-hung houses.

Leave the farm by a stile and continue going north along a rough track that climbs gently for nearly ½ mile. The long summit of Mill Hill is on your R, while L is a beautiful view across the Adur valley to Coombes, with Cissbury Ring on the horizon.

Just before the quarry of the former Shoreham Cement Works, follow the same path as it goes R to meet the road from Shoreham. Turn R and walk south along the road towards Mill Hill. In the valley L lies New Erringham farm, the site of both an old coaching inn on the road to London in the 18th century and a golf club in the 1930s.

Stay on the road until it begins to descend. Enter the car park R, and take time to enjoy both the view and the variety of habitats, including chalk grassland, hawthorn scrub and a new plantation of trees that should be a prominent landmark in the future.

Walk south across the grass, pass the downland reservoir L and continue south, back to the lower car park.

MAP FOR WALK 19
(OS Pathfinder map 1307)

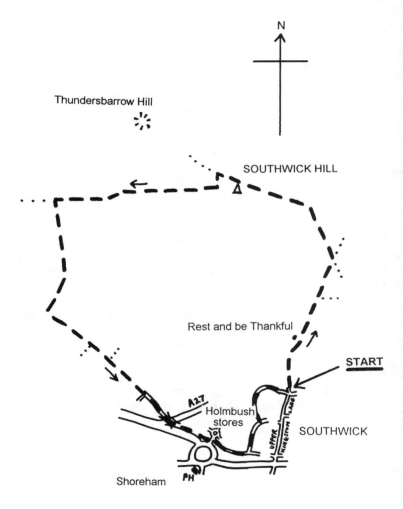

N

Thundersbarrow Hill

SOUTHWICK HILL

Rest and be Thankful

START

A27
Holmbush stores

SOUTHWICK

UPPER KINGSTON LANE

Shoreham

PH

Walk 19

HOLMBUSH VALLEY

Southwick - Southwick Hill - Holmbush Valley - Kingston Broadway - Southwick.

A short, scenic walk with only gentle climbing on the downs north of Shoreham.
Refreshments and toilets in the Holmbush Centre near the end of the walk.

Distance 4 miles   **Climbing** 450ft   **Highest point** 396ft

Start in the rough parking area just beyond the north end of Upper Kingston Lane, SOUTHWICK (*map ref TQ 238066*).

Follow Walk 20 as far as the trig point on the National Trust land at SOUTHWICK HILL.

Continue on the same path for another 60 yards. Then turn L and in 10 yards go R on a path heading west, parallel with the coastline. This is a half-mile, gentle switch-back with good views south and an occasional glimpse of the downs to the west. About 150 yards after a sharp little descent turn L along a path heading south above the east side of the shallow Holmbush Valley.

In a further ½ mile turn L to follow the same path south-east, passing riding stables and a farm R, as you approach the rumbling sound of the A27 trunk road. Cross it by a narrow road bridge and continue down the same road as it passes L the Holmbush superstores in North SHOREHAM.

Emerge on a road between two roundabouts, cross it and go along Kingston Broadway past another superstore, a swimming pool and a parade of shops L. Turn L up Hawkins Road, in 300 yards turn L into Hawkins Crescent and at its end arrive back in Upper Kingston Lane just south of your starting point on the SOUTHWICK side of this boundary road.

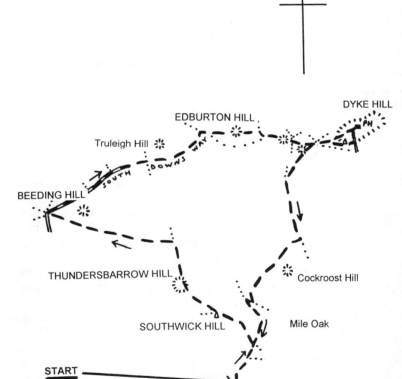

Walk 20

SOUTH DOWNS WAY TO DYKE HILL

Southwick - Southwick Hill - Thundersbarrow - Beeding Hill - Truleigh Hill - Edburton Hill - Perching Hill - Fulking Hill - Dyke Hill - Fulking Hill - Cockroost Hill - Southwick Hill - Southwick.

An energetic switchback of a ramble, where every climb is rewarded by a superb view. The highlight is a four mile section of the South Downs Way, culminating in a visit to the great hillfort on Dyke Hill. The paths are easy to follow and the only part prone to much mud is a short section of bridleway over Southwick Hill. Pub/restaurant and toilets on Dyke Hill.

Distance 11 miles   **Climbing** 1300ft   **Highest point** 711ft

Start in the rough parking area just beyond the north end of Upper Kingston Lane, SOUTHWICK (*map ref TQ 238066*).

Set off along the bridleway leading north on to the downs, and make height steadily, passing the 'Rest and be Thankful' sandstone block L. Soon afterwards the track enters an area of sandy soil owned by the National Trust, and for the next ½ mile may be muddy in wet weather (there are alternative ways through the gorse). Stay on it along the ridge-top as it veers north-west between the gorse. About 60 yards before emerging on open downland you will come across, L, the summit trig point on SOUTHWICK HILL at 396 feet.

The hill to the north-west is THUNDERSBARROW, and you reach it in ½ mile by continuing along the same steadily rising bridleway. The summit is crowned by a hillfort dating from about 500 BC. Carry on along the same path northward. On the horizon ahead are Beeding, Truleigh, Perching, Fulking and Dyke Hills, all of which you are about to conquer!

About ½ mile beyond Thundersbarrow turn L along a distinct bridleway that descends into a valley and climbs out the other side. After 1¼ miles this will bring you to the little car park at 375 feet, just below the top of BEEDING HILL. Six paths converge here, as indicated by the signpost erected by the Society of Sussex Downsmen.

The view is of the hills on the west side of the Adur valley, including Lancing Clump, Steep Down, Cissbury Ring and Steyning Round Hill. Behind lies Chanctonbury, with the villages of Steyning, Bramber and Upper Beeding spread out at your feet.

Now walk north-east on the South Downs Way, as it runs alongside a high lane towards an avenue of conifers. Walk through this, past the Truleigh Hill youth hostel L. Then pass some houses L, close to the summit of Truleigh Hill (708 feet), and continue as a view unfolds of the coast at Brighton and beyond.

After a short descent you will come to a point where a bostal path drops steeply L down the north side of the downs. Here you have a choice. You may either continue along the well-defined South Downs Way or instead take an adventurous alternative over the top of EDBURTON HILL.

For this route, go through the small wooden gate L and do not follow the signposted paths but keep the wire fence R as you ascend over well-grazed turf to the summit at 600 feet. This is an exciting climb with an almost sheer drop L to the tiny hamlet of Edburton.

At the top are a motte and bailey earthwork and splendid views of the Wealden patchwork and the downs to the east as far as Wolstonbury.

Cross a stile to the east and descend above another steep coombe, keeping the same fence R. Near a tall pylon rejoin the South Downs Way and continue along the chalky track as it goes over the top of Perching Hill and passes a Bronze Age barrow L on the way up Fulking Hill. After going through a gate you will see ahead the huge promontory hillfort of DYKE HILL (711ft), acquired by the National Trust in 1995.

The flat-topped summit of Dyke Hill is a massive, rectangular Iron Age hillfort, one of the largest on the South Downs. Its circumference of nearly a mile is formed by a high rampart for some of the way, but in places the steepness of the hillside was sufficient defence from intruders. The highest point, marked by a trig point on top of the southern rampart, gives a good view of the downs and sea to the south, while from the grass in front of the hotel you can see in the west the precipitous north slopes of the downs running away below Fulking, Perching, Edburton and Truleigh Hills and Tottington Mount. To the north lies a broad patchwork of fields, trees and villages, and beyond, the hills of north Sussex and Surrey.

Stay on the Way until it is about to pass the high ramparts of the earthwork L. Climb to the top of them and make for the trig point. Walk east along the rampart, cross a stile to a road, and turn L to reach the pub and restaurant just north of the Devil's Dyke.

After a rest or an exploration of the hillfort, turn to the west, where the downland summits rise sharply from the Weald. Cross a stile by the road, walk across the down and through the ramparts, and go through the gate you encountered earlier. Now turn south-west as you leave the South Downs Way to fork L across the high ground just south of the summit of Fulking Hill. Soon a view of the coast at Worthing opens ahead.

In ½ mile pass through a gate L and take a straight bridleway going due south. In a further ½ mile at a line of transmission wires take a bridleway R leaving at right-angles to pass just north of the dome of Cockroost Hill. At a tall pylon this path veers south-west and begins to descend more steeply into a valley of pylons below Southwick Hill.

Just before reaching the farm buildings at Mile Oak Barn, pass through a gate, turn R, pass another pylon L and at once cross a stile L to enter a sometimes muddy field. Now go beneath the transmission lines along a path that gently ascends the east side of SOUTHWICK HILL. After passing under two more lines of wires you will arrive at a stile on the top of the ridge. Cross it, and you are once more on the bridleway used for your outward journey. Turn L and descend steadily back to Upper Kingston Lane, SOUTHWICK.

MAP FOR WALK 21
(OS Pathfinder maps 1288 and 1307)

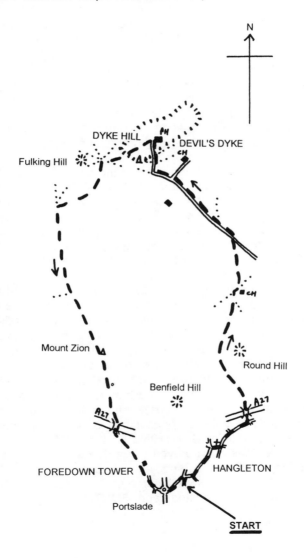

N

DYKE HILL

DEVIL'S DYKE

Fulking Hill

Mount Zion

Benfield Hill

Round Hill

A27

A27

FOREDOWN TOWER

HANGLETON

Portslade

START

Walk 21

THE DYKE RAILWAY

Hangleton - Dyke Hill - Fulking Hill - Mount Zion - Foredown Tower - Hangleton.

The Dyke railway was a branch line that between 1887 and 1938 left the main south coast line at Aldrington and wound its way through Hove and on to the open downs. Its track ended at a point 500ft above sea level, just short of the summit of Dyke Hill. The railway is now only a memory, but part of its route across the downs is now a public walkway and is used for the first section of this walk. This is a very easy ramble on firm ground and gentle gradients, visiting not only the viewpoint on Dyke Hill but also the visitor centre at Foredown Tower. Pub/restaurant and toilets on Dyke Hill.

Distance 7 miles   **Climbing** 600ft   **Highest point** 705ft

Start in Hangleton Valley Drive, close to the Manor at HANGLETON *(map ref TQ 264069).*

Walk north to the road junction, turn R, and then L alongside the large green south of Hangleton parish church.

St Helen's church is a simple but attractive little building of flint. It incorporates both Norman and Early English architecture, and was standing on this hillside about 900 years before any of the surrounding development was dreamed of.

Pass the church L and continue north until you get to a parade of shops. Now set off along the tarmac-surfaced railway path, which begins between the shops and The Downsman public house. Almost at once a view unfolds of the downs as far as Truleigh Hill, and of the course of the old railway, running on ahead around the west side of Hangleton Round Hill.

Stay on the railway path for just over a mile, crossing the A27 by a footbridge on the way. When your path is met by another from the valley L, bear R up the hill towards the white, single-storey clubhouse of the Brighton and Hove golf club.

About 50 yards on, turn L opposite the clubhouse to resume your northward direction. In less than ½ mile you will arrive on the road from Brighton. Cross it, and walk L along the grassy area on the east side of the road.

Soon you will notice a collection of farm buildings in the valley L. These stand on the site of the railway's former terminus, which was about 200 feet below the level of the Dyke Hill summit - the main reason why the railway lost business to motor traffic and had to close in 1938.

Cross the road going R to the clubhouse of the Dyke golf course and continue uphill on the path alongside the road to the summit. After crossing the South Downs Way you will pass the DEVIL'S DYKE.

This is a deep, waterless ravine R, said to have been cut into the downs by the Devil, in an attempt to let in the sea to flood the churches of the Weald. From 1894 to 1909 an aerial cableway supported by two iron towers gave visitors a sensational ride across the ravine.

Carry on to the restaurant and bar near the summit of DYKE HILL, a hillfort with one of the best known and most extensive views in Sussex - *see Walk 20.*

From the hotel walk west along the ridge, passing through the hillfort's ramparts. Go through a gate and take the path L, going south, with a fence L. After about 200 yards bear R across the field, and in ½ mile join two paths from the R and pass through a gate to head south for over two more miles. The path passes over Mount Zion (marked by a trig point L), from which there are good views of Brighton, Hove and Portslade, and then a large dewpond, also L.

Cross the A27 by a bridleway bridge, and continue south to the FOREDOWN TOWER.

This is a visitor centre in a converted water tower. It is open to the public at certain times, and its attractions include a camera obscura.

After the tower, take the second turning L, and descend to the Benfield valley by Fox Way. At the roundabout go straight on by Hangleton Lane into HANGLETON to complete your walk.

Walk 22

BELOW DYKE HILL

Dyke Hill - Devil's Dyke - Poynings - Fulking - Fulking Hill - Dyke Hill

An exhilarating walk that starts at its highest point. Some of the paths can be muddy, but otherwise the route is a pleasant one, visiting a magnificent downland church and ending with a fine, exposed climb up the northern scarp of the downs. Pub/restaurant and toilets on Dyke Hill, and pubs in Poynings and Fulking.

Distance 4½ miles   **Climbing** 550ft   **Highest point** 700ft

Start in the car park south of the DEVIL'S DYKE Hotel *(map ref TQ 258110).*

Find the gap in the south side of the grass bank surrounding the car park and walk south for 20 yards to pick up a bridleway heading east along the northern lip of the DEVIL'S DYKE, *described in Walk 21.*

In 400 yards a L fork goes up to the hillfort ramparts, but you must take the R fork and steadily descend north-eastwards. There is a splendid view of Newtimber Hill, and of its satellite West Hill, with Saddlescombe nestling below. Soon your path bears L and gives a distant view of the Weald, including Hurstpierpoint, just behind Newtimber Hill, and Poynings at your feet.

Go through a small gate and now drop down more steeply through a wood that conceals a short, muddy stretch. Out of the wood, bear R to walk between fences and arrive at a lane opposite Dyke Farm House. Turn R to enter POYNINGS. Go past the Royal Oak pub, and continue along the path known as 'Cora's Walk' that is raised above the road, R. Eventually this will bring you through an archway to Holy Trinity church.

MAP FOR WALK 22
(OS Pathfinder map 1288)

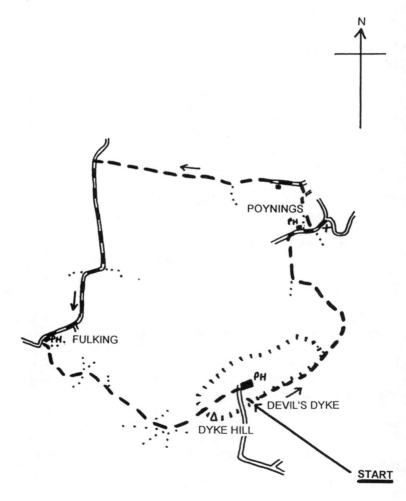

N

POYNINGS

FULKING

DEVIL'S DYKE

DYKE HILL

START

Poynings parish church was built in the 14th century. A grey, flint, cruciform building, it stands solidly atop a hillock overlooking the Weald. Inside you are in for a surprise, for all is lightness and space, with large, clear windows and tall, graceful pillars and arches.

Cross back over the road to Judy's and Merilees's seats, and walk back along Cora's Walk to just past the Forge Garage. Now go through a kissing gate R to take a path that keeps close to a high, wooden fence R. In 200 yards bear R and cross a stream. Then go L opposite a white painted cottage with a weather-vane.

Now walk north beside a chestnut fence until you emerge in concrete-surfaced Mill Lane. Turn L, and pass Mill House, L. When the track ends by a sewage plant R, continue west along a path with a running stream L. After a further 150 yards cross a small bridge over the stream and head for the top of a small rise across the field. Go over a stile and note fine views of Wolstonbury and Newtimber Hills in the east, and the high, downland range to the south. The summits, L to R are Dyke, Fulking, Perching, Edburton and Truleigh Hills.

Continue to walk west over the highest ground as you cross the middle of a very large field that is often cultivated. Beyond another stile proceed in the same direction, with a wood R and some glasshouses L, until you arrive by way of a further stile in Clappers Lane. Turn L along the lane to its end in the village of FULKING.

Then go straight on (west) through the village street, past the shop R, and downhill to the Shepherd and Dog pub L. Walk through the pub's car park to find a footpath between hedges that soon bears R and heads up hill. Cross a stile and continue the climb through scrub and on to the open downland of the Fulking Escarpment (National Trust).

At a meeting of five paths halfway up the hill, go straight ahead to continue the climb, pausing to take in the view of Fulking and Poynings. Go through a gate near the top, and then head directly for the restaurant on DYKE HILL where you began.

MAP FOR WALK 23

(OS Pathfinder map 1288)

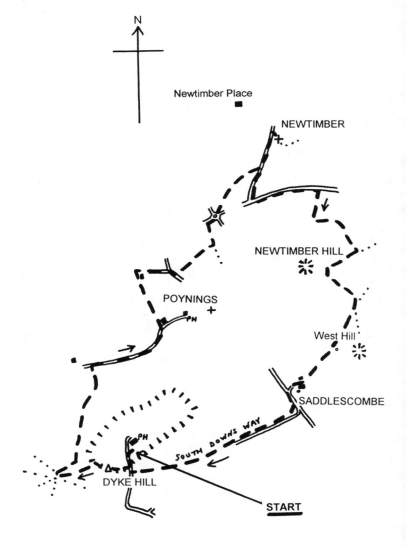

Walk 23

NEWTIMBER HILL

Dyke Hill - Poynings - Newtimber church - Newtimber Hill - Saddlescombe - Dyke Hill

Highlights of this walk are the extensive views from the hillfort on Dyke Hill and from Newtimber Hill, both properties of the National Trust. There is likely to be much mud in wet weather just before Saddlescombe. Pub, restaurant and toilets on Dyke Hill.

Distance 7½ miles   **Climbing** 860ft   **Highest point** 711ft

Start in the car park south of the DEVIL'S DYKE Hotel *(map ref TQ 258110).*

Turn L along the roadside path for 50 yards, and then cross the road to go over a stile and on to the trig point on the southern rampart of the DYKE HILL Iron Age hillfort (711ft).

The western view extends along the downs to Chanctonbury and distant Tegleaze, highest of the Sussex downs. To the north you might pick out Blackdown and the ridges around Handcross Hill; to the south-east the mast on White-hawk Hill; and in the south-west you may just see the outline of the Isle of Wight.

Walk along the rampart to its western end above Fulking. Then descend L by a chalk path, and continue west across springy turf. Keep close to the escarpment for about 200 yards, and then find a bridleway that is a bostal path descending into a steep-sided coombe R.

Drop down steeply below the Devil's Dyke Hotel as the path winds down to the foot of the hill. At the bottom go through a small gate and follow the path north to the road, just R of a house with a windpump. Now turn R along the lane towards POYNINGS. As soon as you enter the village, take a footpath L in front of a brick-and-flint barn. Go through a gate and continue north on a raised path across a field.

In ¼ mile cross a stream, and at the sewage works turn R. Soon you are on a concrete track that passes the Mill House R. Arriving at a road, turn R for 50 yards and find a footpath L through the school playground. This continues across a field with a hedge L. Newtimber Hill is now prominent ahead. Cross a babbling stream fed by nearby springs and continue across the field towards the base of Newtimber Hill. The springs are on your R, marked by pock marks in the meadow.

At the end of the next field turn L and follow the hedge until you emerge on the road at a roundabout. Go over the stile on the opposite side of the roundabout and cross further stiles and fields, all the time heading north east. Soon you will see 17th century Newtimber Place L, and the church ahead. Arriving in the lane, turn L to visit NEWTIMBER church.

Set in a truly peaceful corner of rural Sussex, the church of St John the Baptist is basically Early English but was heavily restored by the Victorians. Its tower dates only from 1839. The Old Rectory north of the churchyard also is Victorian.

Now go back south along the lane as far as its junction with the A281 Horsham road. Turn L and walk beside the road for about 600 yards. Newtimber Hill is on your R and ahead is Wolstonbury. On reaching a National Trust sign at a field boundary R, take the bridle path R into the woods.

Don't worry - your route is not straight up! The path soon bears L and ascends the hill by a long slog around the north and east sides. Once through a gate near the top, turn R on to open downland and make the gentle climb to the flat summit of NEWTIMBER HILL - not marked by a trig point.

The eastern view embraces Wolstonbury (with Hurstpierpoint College to its L), Jack and Jill windmills, Ditchling Beacon and distant Beddingham Hill with the masts. South, beyond West Hill (an outlier of Newtimber), is the coast, while west the view is dominated by Dyke Hill and the downs around masted Truleigh.

Now head across short downland turf for the top of West Hill, but after 200 yards bear R to follow a grass path

Now head across short downland turf for the top of West Hill, but after 200 yards bear R to follow a grass path coming in diagonally from the L. This heads towards the Devil's Dyke, and after 100 yards passes a dewpond L. Descend ever more steeply, and in the muddy corner of a field near the bottom go through a gate to join the South Downs Way and enter SADDLESCOMBE.

Follow the bridleway signs through this isolated farming hamlet, cross the road and now watch for the South Downs Way signs as you climb out of the valley over downland and through scrub all the way back to the top of DYKE HILL. Once on the road, turn R to regain your starting point.

Looking back to Saddlescombe *(Walk 23)*

MAP FOR WALK 24
(OS Pathfinder map 1288)

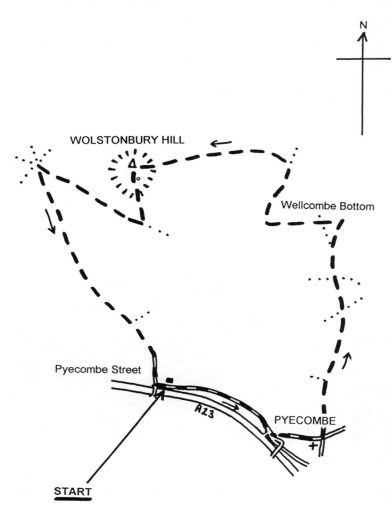

Walk 24

WOLSTONBURY

Pyecombe Street - Pyecombe - Wellcombe Bottom - Wolstonbury Hill - Pyecombe Street

A short walk to the finest viewpoint in this book. It is best done on a clear day, in high summer or a day of hard frost, as some of the route is on bridleways that get very muddy in winter. The Plough pub/restaurant is at the southern end of Pyecombe.

Distance 3½ miles   **Climbing** 480ft   **Highest point** 677ft

Start at the layby on the former route of the Brighton-London road north of PYECOMBE village, just before Pyecombe Street and close to the bridleway bridge over the present A23 *(map ref TQ 284129).*

Walk south along the roadside path, parallel with the new road. In 500 yards turn L, and ascend Church Hill along the South Downs Way to visit Pyecombe church.

The church, dedicated to the Transfiguration, is a small, simple building of flint covered by pebbledash. Most of the fabric is Norman, but the tower, with its familiar 'Sussex cap', is 13th century. Its prize possession is a deep, cylindrical font of decorated lead - one of only three in Sussex that survived the Civil War.

Immediately after passing the end of the churchyard wall go L up The Wyshe, which soon deteriorates into a bridleway heading north, uphill. Keep straight on at two cross-paths. The second one provides a good view of Wolstonbury, with Hurstpierpoint below and to its R.

Stay on the broad track for a further 300 yards, as it now goes downhill and into the woods. Then go L along another bridleway that eventually emerges from the woods on to grassland near the base of Wellcombe Bottom. Bear R as the path winds around the end of the bottom and then climbs a little to the long shoulder coming down from the top of the hill.

Now go through a gate into National Trust property and walk up the obvious footpath all the way to the ramparts on the WOLSTONBURY Iron Age hillfort. Walk R along the ramparts for wonderful views to the east, north and west, before making for the trig point in the centre, at 677 feet.

The Wolstonbury earthwork is unusual in that the rampart is constructed outside the ditch. Within it are a dew-pond and a number of bumps and hollows. In the east are Jack and Jill windmills and Ditchling Beacon beyond them. To the north is the patchwork of the Sussex Weald, with Hurst-pierpoint, Hassocks, Burgess Hill, Keymer and Ditchling all prominent within four miles and in the foreground the red brick 18th century facade of Danny. The western view is of the downland range, extending from Newtimber Hill, past Dyke Hill and Truleigh Hill, with Cissbury Ring and Chanctonbury Ring in the distance. To the south you may see the tower blocks of Brighton, through a cleft in the downs.

Leave Wolstonbury by the path going south from the summit (towards Brighton). In 300 yards meet a bridleway and go R, downhill in the direction of the Weald, keeping a fence on your L. Stay on this path for nearly ½ mile, and at a National Trust sign go through a gate L to find a bridleway that will lead you in three quarters of a mile back to PYECOMBE Street.

Walk 25

PYECOMBE AND WOLSTONBURY

Patcham - Sweet Hill - Pyecombe Street - Wolstonbury - Pyecombe - Chattri - Patcham

A fine walk on gentle gradients that is full of surprises. Pub in Patcham village

Distance 10 miles   **Climbing** 1100ft   **Highest point** 677ft

Start at the blocked up eastern end of Vale Road, PATCHAM *(map ref TQ 299092)*.

Cross the A23, and go straight on under the Mill Road railway bridge. Walk on the R grass verge for 100 yards, and then turn R to walk under the A27. Turn R again, and after the Southern Water gate find a gate L that leads to a bridleway climbing the side of Sweet Hill.

Pass downland reservoirs R and L, and then go through a metal gate R to walk north with scrub growth L. Continue the climb, pausing to look back for a good view over Brighton, with the racecourse, the Whitehawk Hill mast and Patcham windmill the chief landmarks. On your R notice a recently restored dewpond.

Just before the rounded top of West Hill in the National Trust's Newtimber Hill property go through a gate and continue north, keeping a fence R. Here there is an extensive view along the line of downs as far as Chanctonbury, and soon Wolstonbury comes into view ahead, R.

Leave the National Trust land by a small gate leading to a bridleway that heads at first in the direction of Wolstonbury. Gradually this descends with a fence R to the northern part of Pyecombe at Wayfield Farm. At the corner of the field go over a stile and cross the A23 cutting by a bridleway bridge to PYECOMBE.

Now go up Pyecombe street past flint cottages, and continue as it becomes a track. At a fork take the lower path

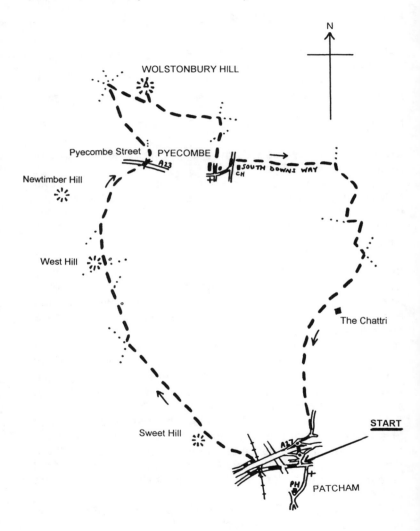

between hedges, which runs parallel with the road. In about ½ mile go through a wooden gate R on to the National Trust land of WOLSTONBURY. Take the path that climbs the side of the hill, keeping a fence R until just before the summit of the path. Then turn L along the footpath to the top of the hill. The view is the finest in this part of the downs - *see Walk 24.*

Retrace your steps to the path over the shoulder, and turn L. Continue alongside the fence R, and notice Jack and Jill windmills on the hill opposite. At a crosspaths go R, to walk south along a muddy bridleway for ½ mile down to PYECOMBE's southern part.

Reaching the crossroads go R to visit the church *(see Walk 24)*, but then return to take the L road (School Lane), which is also part of the South Downs Way. Turn L along the path beside A273 for 100 yards, and then cross the road to continue on the South Downs Way as it climbs through the Pyecombe golf course.

At the end of the golf course turn R and follow this track as it winds over the hill to the south. Just over the ridge of this hill turn L, and in 200 yards go R again towards a clump of trees on the horizon. You will pass them R after making a short L and R diversion. Keeping a fence R, descend gradually towards Brighton and Hove, and you will pass L the dome of The Chattri, a fine memorial to Indian soldiers who gave their lives in the Great War.

Just over ½ mile after The Chattri go through a gate under transmission lines and head across a field in the direction of Brighton. Go through a further gate to join a lane descending to PATCHAM. Just before the A27 cutting go R and descend to a roundabout. Cross the road, continue south over the road bridge and still south at the next roundabout. Then turn R down Vale Road to regain your starting point.

MAP FOR WALK 26
(OS Pathfinder maps 1288 and 1307)

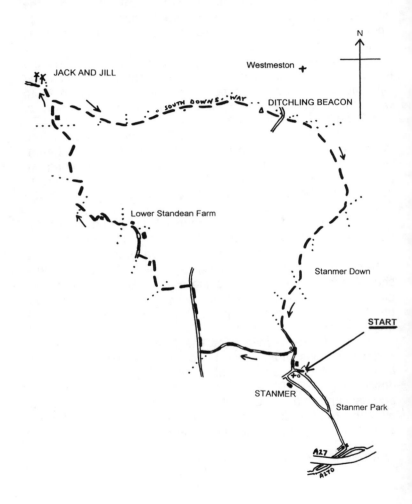

Walk 26

MILLS AND BEACON

Stanmer - Lower Standean - Jack and Jill - Ditchling Beacon - Moon's Bottom - Stanmer.

A hilly but mainly firm walk across unspoiled downland, taking in the famous Jack and Jill windmills, a fine 2½ mile stretch of the South Downs Way and extensive views from the top of Ditchling Beacon, the highest point in East Sussex. No pubs along this route, but there is a cafe/restaurant at Stanmer.

Distance 9½ miles   **Climbing** 1060ft   **Highest point** 814ft

Start at the car park in STANMER village, just east of the pond by the church (*map ref TQ 337096*).

Stanmer is a tiny village within the Brighton borough, set in beautiful parkland with a large early 18th century manor house, a 19th century flint church with a slender spire and several flint faced cottages.
Turn R out of the car park, pass the well house L next to the church and go R again up the village street. Just past the last row of cottages turn L at a duck pond and walk up a quiet lane, signposted 'No Through Road'. Stay on it for nearly a mile, as an ever widening view behind you extends to Firle Beacon in the south-east and Newmarket Hill to the south. Just after going between the white Upper Lodges, bear R through a picnic area and then R along the verge of the Brighton-Ditchling road for ½ mile.
Immediately after passing under transmission lines cross a stile L and go down a footpath that leads at first west, and then swings north into a valley dominated by a large barn. Pass the barn L and go through a gate to continue the descent until you meet a road through the valley bottom. Turn R along this lane and walk through Lower Standean Farm.
About 150 yards after the last farm building go straight on at a crosspaths, on a bridleway that leads into a shallow

valley. Pass a small brick-and-flint barn L, and climb out of the valley. Bear L through a gate, and at the next gate go R through a copse. Now bear R and head for another gate north-west across the field. Go through it, and turn L to walk beside a fence L. In 100 yards follow the same path as it now heads north, keeping the same fence L. In 250 yards go through a small gate and turn L into a valley for another 200 yards. Then take the wide bridleway R that heads generally north towards the two windmills, skirting Pyecombe golf course L.

At the end of the golf course go straight on at a crosspaths, pass through New Barn Farm, and on joining the South Downs Way turn L for a closer look at JACK AND JILL.

Jack, a brick tower mill, was erected in 1866 next to the roundhouse of the post mill it replaced. It received a face-lift in 1973, when it secured the title role in the film 'The Black Mill', starring Michael Caine. Jill is a white-painted, weather-boarded post mill, first erected in Brighton early in the 19th century. In 1852 it was towed on a trolley to its present site by horses and oxen, after encroaching development on Brighton's hills had literally taken the wind out of its sails. Both mills are now maintained in good repair by the Jack and Jill Mills Pres-ervation Society, and Jill is usually open on Sundays in the summer.

Before you leave the mills, be sure to see the view from the car park.

It extends west to Wolstonbury and the line of downs beyond, and north to the downs and sandy ridges of Surrey. At your feet lies the village of Clayton (and the nearest pub!) while the larger towns of Hassocks and Burgess Hill are further north.

Now head east along an excellent stretch of the South Downs Way, with firm walking, fine views over Weald, downs and coast, and several well-preserved dewponds. After two miles, just after passing above Ditchling village, you will arrive near the summit of DITCHLING BEACON (813ft), just R of the Way.

The view from the summit is one of the best in East Sussex. In the west, you may see Worthing, and to its R the downland peaks of Dyke Hill, Truleigh (with the masts), Chanctonbury and much nearer Wolstonbury. To the north the spire of Hurstpierpoint church is prominent, as are the communities of Hassocks, Keymer, Burgess Hill and Haywards Heath. In the east the downs roll on to Streat Hill and Blackcap, while in the distance stand rounded Windover Hill, nose-like Firle Beacon and the wedged shape of Seaford Head, nearest the sea. South you may see the downs around Newmarket Hill and the stands on Brighton racecourse.

Continue east down to the car park, cross the road and go through a small gate to resume the South Downs Way for another 600 yards. Then leave it by a gate behind some bushes R, and walk along a bridleway across a large field. First this heads south-east towards Seaford Head, but soon it veers south, to take you into a shallow coombe and out the other side. About 300 yards from the base of the valley go through a gate R and descend once more, into the peaceful, winding valley known as Moon's Bottom.

Walk through the valley for about ¼ mile, pass through another gate, and in a further 200 yards find a pair of gates R, on the edge of a wood. Beyond these, fork R up a path that climbs through the trees. At the top go straight on along a flinty track that now descends steadily to arrive in less than a mile back at your starting point in STANMER.

MAP FOR WALK 27
(OS Pathfinder map 1307)

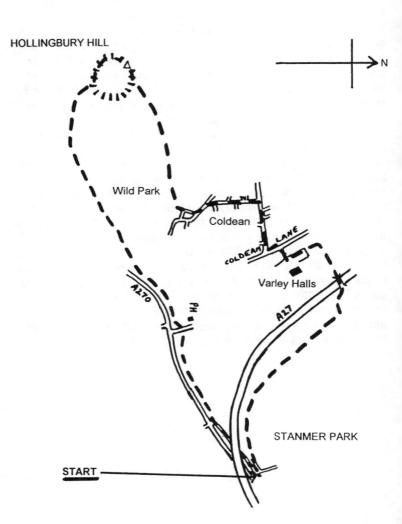

HOLLINGBURY HILL

N

Wild Park

Coldean

COLDEAN LANE

Varley Halls

A270

A27

PH

STANMER PARK

START

Walk 27

HOLLINGBURY

Stanmer Park - Wild Park - Hollingbury Hill - Coldean - Stanmer Park

The deep Wild Park valley and the Hollingbury hillfort form a green oasis amid several Brighton housing estates. This short walk passes through pleasant woodland in both directions and includes a steep climb of Hollingbury Hill. There is a pub (The Hiker's Rest) near the start.

Distance 3½ miles **Climbing** 450ft **Highest point** 584ft

Start in the car park at the south end of STANMER PARK *(map ref TQ 343086)*, reached from the single-track lane off A270 Lewes Road.

Go through the kissing gate behind the toilet block and turn R along the lane, under the A27 flyover. Then take a footpath parallel with the road L to climb with some trees R. Soon you enter a wood, and keep going west to drop down and cross Coldean Lane near the Hiker's Rest pub.

Now walk west beside A270 on a pedestrian/cycle path, past Woburn Place R and through a landscaped area of grass, trees and bushes. Arriving at the entrance to the Wild Park, make for the wooded hill opposite, and begin to climb it, first by some steps and then up a steep slope through the trees. At a crosspaths turn L and continue the climb. (There are many paths up the side of Hollingbury Hill. If you get lost just keep making for higher ground until you get to the top!)

The path you should be on veers R to head north. When the woods begin to thin out fork R and in about 20 yards go L to continue the climb along a broader path. In another 100 yards turn R along a flint track and emerge on a golf course. Stay on this track, keeping the golf course L. At a large bank protecting one of the greens turn L to leave the track, skirt the green L and on its opposite side turn R to walk up hill to a collection of concrete posts on the rampart of HOLLINGBURY HILL's hillfort. Turn L, walk along the top of the rampart to the trig point (584ft) at its north-west corner.

The hillfort dates from the middle Iron Age (250-50 BC). Its ramparts are still impressive, but the large area they enclose is rather overgrown with gorse and brambles. On a clear day several familiar hills line the western horizon. From R to L they are Wolstonbury, Newtimber Hill, Dyke Hill, Truleigh Hill, Chanctonbury, Cissbury and Highdown. When it is exceptionally clear you may see Shanklin Down on the Isle of Wight. South lies Brighton, dominated by the race hill, while to the east are Cliffe Hill and Mount Caburn beyond Lewes, and Newmarket Hill with its crowning mast.

Continue round the rampart for a further 100 yards, and leave it by a path L where the golf course seems to end. Suddenly the course reappears, and you must cross a fairway, enter a wood and, about 20 yards inside it, turn L along a broad path. In about 50 yards emerge from the wood, and continue to walk east with open down L and bushes and trees R, at the top of the steep slope above the Wild Park.

Keep on walking east, and drop down past a wooden mast into a road called The Meads. At its end turn L into Reeves Hill, and next R into Nanson Road. At a T-junction go R into Hawkhurst Road, and follow this down to its junction with the former A27, Coldean Lane. Now turn L for 100 yards and then cross the road and walk up the approach road to the Varley Halls of Residence.

Turn L through the car park in front of Chalvington Close. Continue along a track for 20 yards, and then find a footpath going R, up hill through the trees to a footbridge over the A27 trunk road. Cross it and continue up the bank on the other side. Go through a kissing gate and walk east into the wood for about 20 yards. Then turn R, and stay on a broad track that heads south, just inside the edge of the wood. When the trees begin to clear carry on down the same path and follow it as it curves L, following the line of the A27 cutting. At a crosspaths, looking across to Sussex University, go straight on, steeply down hill into STANMER PARK.

Walk 28

SIX MILES ALONG THE WAY

Falmer - St Mary's Farm - Streathill Farm - Streat Hill - Plumpton Plain - Blackcap - Balmer Down - Newmarket - Newmarket Plantation - Falmer

A splendid downland walk along well-defined paths, including more than six miles of the South Downs Way and wide views of the Weald and downs. The New-market is a family restaurant , and there is a pub in the northern half of Falmer.

Distance 10½ miles **Climbing** 850ft **Highest point** 677ft

Start by the north side of the village pond in the southern part of FALMER *(map ref TQ 354087)* .

Go to the lane that passes the front of the church and walk north along East Street. Then turn L along a footpath behind a high brick wall as far as the footbridge over A27. Cross the bridge and turn R to pass the flint cottages of Middle Street. Then go L up Ridge Road past the Old Forge Barn R. At a fork by some ruined farm buildings, keep L on the surfaced lane and descend to the red brick houses of St Mary's Farm.

After passing the last house in the farm bear R, and about 50 yards further on turn L to climb steadily north, above peaceful Shambledean Bottom L. Arriving at a large clump of trees L, look back for a good view of Newmarket Hill (with the mast) and the sprawling University of Sussex. In a further ½ mile pass the brick buildings of Streathill Farm L and soon emerge on the South Downs Way at Streat Hill.

Walk R along the Way for just over a mile. Soon a view unfolds over the Weald, with Plumpton Agricultural College prominent below, while away to the east you might spot the nose-like Firle Beacon. Beyond flat-topped Plumpton Plain the South Downs Way leaves the ridge to head south.

MAP FOR WALK 28
(OS Pathfinder maps 1288 and 1307)

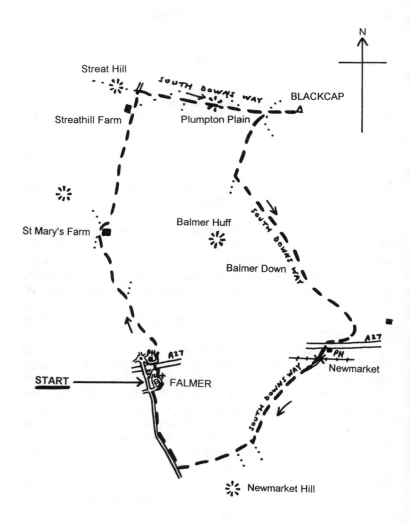

N

Streat Hill

SOUTH DOWNS WAY

BLACKCAP

Streathill Farm

Plumpton Plain

St Mary's Farm

Balmer Huff

SOUTH DOWNS WAY

Balmer Down

A27
PH
Newmarket

START → FALMER

PH A27

SOUTH DOWNS WAY

Newmarket Hill

Do not follow it yet, but go through the gate ahead and walk up the grassy slope to the viewpoint on BLACKCAP (677ft).

To the east the nearest hill is Mount Harry, site of the Battle of Lewes in 1264. Just beyond it are Cliffe Hill and Mount Caburn; Windover Hill and Firle Beacon are on the horizon. South-east are the Ouse valley and Seaford Head.

Retrace your steps to the South Downs Way and now walk south for just over ½ mile. Just before the path drops down to a line of pylons turn L to walk south-east, still on the Way. Pass under the transmission lines and walk on over Balmer Down. After a mile on this track turn R at the SD Way signpost and head down hill, between fences, towards Bunkershill Plantation. At the valley bottom follow the path as it climbs and winds steeply through the wood. Emerging at the top of Long Hill, walk south-west down hill towards A27.

Go through the gate at the bottom and walk R along the tarmac path beside the road for 150 yards. Just after Housedean Farm R, follow the South Downs Way L, across the bridge and down the roadway L. Just before arriving back at the main road, pass through a gate ahead and continue between fences for 400 yards. Then go through another gate to pass under the railway, and then immediately turn L along side the railway embankment for 80 yards. Go R for 50 yards then L, up hill through the trees to emerge on a track leading to the top of Newmarket Hill.

After passing the trees at the top, leave the South Downs Way to go R along a grassy bridleway that first doubles back along the other side of the fence and then bears L beside a hedgerow and makes for the Falmer-Rottingdean road ½ mile away to the east. Follow it all the way to the road, noting a panoramic view R of the hills along the downland ridge - Ditchling Beacon, Streat Hill, Blackcap and Mount Harry. Turn R at the road and descend to FALMER. Turn R into Park Street to get back to the pond where you began.

The flint-built village is worth a wander if you have time. The church of St Laurence dates from 1815 and was built in the Norman style. The village pub, the Swan Inn, is across the footbridge beyond the A27 cutting.

SOUTH SUSSEX RAMBLES

1998 update

The text was correct at the time of publication, but a few changes have occurred since!

Please amend as follows:

Page 9   *Food & drink at about half way.* Delete 28 and 34 (see below).

Page 25   *Walk 5.* The Lemon Tree café is now the Blue Bird café.

Page 101   *Walk 28.* The South Downs Way was rerouted in 1997 to cross A27 by a bridge instead of the dangerous crossing at the Newmarket restaurant. The overall distance is about the same. Please delete page 101 and stick over it the new page opposite.

Page 117   *Walk 34.* Sadly, the Royal Oak pub has now closed, and is a private house.

Colin Ulph
January 1998

Do not follow it yet, but go through the gate ahead and walk up the grassy slope to the viewpoint on BLACKCAP (677ft).

To the east the nearest green hill is Mount Harry, where the Battle of Lewes was fought in 1264. Just beyond it are Cliffe Hill and Mount Caburn, with Windover Hill and Firle Beacon on the horizon. To the south-east are the broad Ouse valley and Seaford Head.

Retrace your steps to the South Downs Way and now walk south for just over ½ mile. Just before the path drops down to a line of pylons turn L to walk south-east, still on the South Downs Way. Pass under the transmission lines and walk on over Balmer Down. After 1½ miles on this track reach the bottom of a valley. Do not go through the metal gate just before a barn, but take a path leading half R over the lower slopes of the hill towards a small wood.

Continue to climb through the wood, and as you leave it bear R to follow the South Downs Way south-west as it descends to the A27 trunk road. Follow the signs across the road to the Newmarket restaurant. Walk up the lane between this and the petrol station, under the railway arch and R up the lower slopes of Newmarket Hill. Walk past the plantation R, decimated in the 'hurricane' of 1987.

Now leave the South Downs Way through a gate R, for a grassy bridleway that first doubles back along the other side of the fence and then bears L beside a hedgerow and makes for the Falmer-Rottingdean road ½ mile away to the east.

Follow it all the way to the road, noting a panoramic view R of the hills along the downland ridge - Ditchling Beacon, Streat Hill, Blackcap and Mount Harry. Turn R at the road and descend to FALMER. Turn R into Park Street to get back to the pond where you began.

The flint-built village is worth a wander if you have time. The church of St Laurence dates from 1815 and was built in the Norman style. The village pub, the Swan Inn, is across the footbridge beyond the A27 cutting.

MAP FOR WALKS 29 AND 30
(OS Pathfinder map 1307)

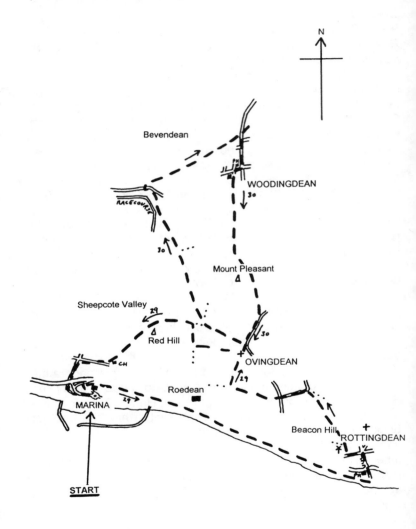

N

Bevendean

WOODINGDEAN

30

RACECOURSE

30

Mount Pleasant
△

Sheepcote Valley
29

△
Red Hill

30

✝
OVINGDEAN

CH

MARINA

29

Roedean

29

Beacon Hill

✝
ROTTINGDEAN

START

Walk 29

THE UNDERCLIFF

Brighton Marina - Rottingdean - Beacon Hill - Ovingdean - Cattle Hill - Red Hill - Brighton Marina

An easy walk with just two short, steep climbs. The outward journey is a two mile walk along the Undercliff promenade, and the return is over the downs, incorporating a visit to the flint village of Ovingdean. If the weather is rough and the tide is high, be prepared to dodge the waves as they hit the sea wall! The ramble can be extended to more than 10 miles by picking up Walk 30 at Ovingdean and walking to Woodingdean and back across the downs. There are pubs and restaurants at both the Marina and Rottingdean.

Distance 6 miles   **Climbing** 580ft   **Highest point** 350ft

Start in the large car park next to the supermarket at BRIGHTON MARINA (*map ref TQ 336033*).

Leave the car park at its western end and climb the steps to the Undercliff walk. Turn R and walk just over two miles to Rottingdean, passing the Marina village R, below sheer, crumbly cliffs with their streaks of black flint.

Just below a block of flats turn L and climb the steps to the White Horse Hotel, ROTTINGDEAN. Cross the main road at the traffic lights and walk north up Rottingdean High Street, where there are pubs and tea rooms. Turn L into Nevill Road, and continue up a rough track. Near the top turn R into Sheep Walk, which becomes a bridleway going north-west over the downs. Pass Rottingdean's black smock mill L.

The mill was built in 1802, and ground corn for the village until 1881. Its shell is now maintained by a local pres-ervation society.

Continue north-west over Beacon Hill, past the pitch and putt course and a dried up dewpond L. Arriving in Beacon Hill road, turn L and descend west, crossing Greenways in the valley. Go over the stile opposite, and climb up a footpath for

150 yards, keeping a fence R. Just before the highest point of the path cross a stile R and continue with the fence L. At a circular, brick well-head turn R, drop down into a muddy field and go through a gate into OVINGDEAN churchyard. You enter the church porch beneath a massive 1000 year old yew tree.

The church of St Wulstan dates from just after the Norman conquest. It has a heavy, square tower, topped with a 'Sussex cap'. Inside it boasts three graceful arches between the nave and chancel, and a charming little chapel adjoining the chancel.

Leave the church by the lych gate to the east, and go over the stile in the wall to find a footpath that climbs the field with the churchyard wall L. Climb over the steps in the wall ahead, and continue to walk west, keeping a fence close R. Over another stile continue over the top of Cattle Hill, noting Roedean school and the Marina L.

In the next valley join a south-north footpath and go R on it for ½ mile. Then fork L to join a bridleway going west over Red Hill, which has a trig point and a golf course on its summit. Once over the top you cannot miss the ugly scar of the Sheepcote Valley rubbish infill site.

Now follow the track as it descends south-west past the clubhouse of the East Brighton golf club and merges with a road that takes you to some traffic lights. Here turn L and follow the signs down to the car park at the MARINA.

Walk 30

OVINGDEAN

Woodingdean - Mount Pleasant - Ovingdean - Brighton race-course - Woodingdean

A short, easy walk on mainly firm tracks, visiting the little Norman church at Ovingdean. There's a pub at the crossroads in Woodingdean.

Distance 4½ miles   **Climbing** 420ft   **Highest point** 540ft

Start in the rough parking area and picnic site in Falmer Road, WOODINGDEAN, about 200 yards north of its junction with Bexhill Road *(map ref TQ 356064).*

Turn L out of the car park and walk south as far as the traffic lights. Turn R into Warren Road, and in 150 yards go L into Old Parish Lane. Pass the school buildings and continue south along a broad track that gives a distant view of the windmill at Rottingdean.

After skirting the summit of Mount Pleasant, return to civilisation at a made-up road. Turn R to descend on the roadside path, and then R again down a lane between flint walls. At the bottom go L into Greenways, and in 20 yards turn R to visit OVINGDEAN church, *described in Walk 29.*

Leave the church by the lych gate and turn L along Greenways. When after 20 yards this bears R, go straight on through a farm. At a fork after ¼ mile go R into a valley and 150 yards further on continue going north as the track climbs steadily, with a golf course L. Carry on when the racecourse comes in L, and arrive on Warren Road, WOODINGDEAN.

Now turn L along the grass north of the racecourse, and cross Warren Road opposite the western end of Downland Road. Pass the enclosed reservoir R, and in 20 yards turn R along a track that leads behind the Downland Road houses for nearly a mile, back to your starting point.

MAP FOR WALK 31
(OS Pathfinder maps 1307 and 1308)

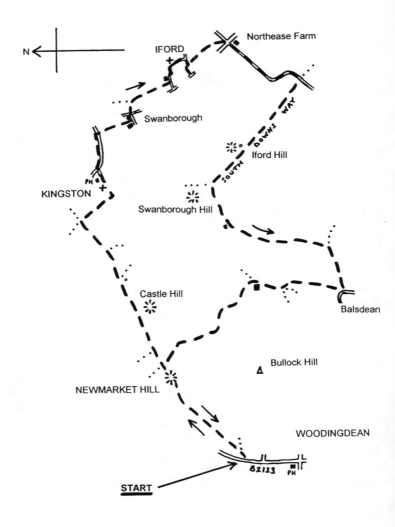

N

Northease Farm

IFORD

Swanborough

SOUTH DOWNS WAY

Iford Hill

KINGSTON

PH

Swanborough Hill

Castle Hill

Balsdean

Bullock Hill

NEWMARKET HILL

WOODINGDEAN

B2123 PH

START

Walk 31

EAST OF NEWMARKET

Woodingdean - Newmarket Hill - Castle Hill - Kingston-near-Lewes - Swanborough - Iford - Northease Farm - Iford Hill - Balsdean - Falmer Bottom - Castle Hill Nature Reserve - Newmarket Hill - Woodingdean

A superb walk on mainly firm ground across some of the unspoiled rolling downland beyond Newmarket Hill, east of Brighton. There are visits to two ancient churches and spectacular views of the Ouse valley. There are pubs in Kingston and at the crossroads in Woodingdean.

Distance 12 miles **Climbing** 1200ft **Highest point** 645ft

Start in the rough parking area and picnic site in Falmer Road, WOODINGDEAN, about 200 yards north of its junction with Bexhill Road *(map ref TQ 356064).*

Take the L of two tracks and set off north-east in the direction of the mast near the top of NEWMARKET HILL (645ft). Walk past the mast R, and pause by the dried up dewpond R to take in the view.
To the west is Brighton, with the racecourse stands prominent. Beyond it the coastline stretches west to Worthing. In the north-west is Hollingbury Hill, and to its R are the wooded Stanmer estate with the mansion and tall-spired church, the sprawling buildings of Sussex University and the square tower of Falmer church. North-east are the downs around Lewes, and ½ mile away east is Castle Hill, your next target. To the south-east are Falmer Bottom, Bullock Hill (topped by a trig point) and Seaford Head, guarding the coast in the distance.
Continue along the track over Castle Hill, as the South Downs Way joins just before the final ascent to the summit. Shortly beyond the top you will notice near the path to the north-east some gorse-filled depressions, one filled with water.

Pass them R, and now leave the South Downs Way by going straight on downhill in the direction of Lewes, now visible in the valley. Soon Kingston village comes into view below, and the chalky bostal path winds down steeply to enter it. On joining a made-up lane, at once turn R to descend along a bridleway behind the houses. Continue in the same direction when the path becomes 'Church Lane', and again past the tennis courts L. Then follow it through the trees to arrive at the gate of KINGSTON church.

Dedicated to St Pancras, this is a small, flint building with a slender west tower. Although much restored, it is basically an early 14th century church in the Decorated style, and inside it is light, spacious and very beautiful.

From the south porch go through a tapsell gate and then L down the village street. Just past The Juggs 15th century pub, turn R along Wellgreen Lane, signposted 'Newhaven'. In ¼ mile find a footpath R that leads over a small rise to Swanborough, giving fine views of the downland peaks R and the Ouse valley L, dominated by Lewes and its Norman castle keep.

Walk through Swanborough Farm, turn L and soon emerge on the Lewes-Newhaven road. Cross the road and a stile on the far side to find the footpath to Iford. Proceed south-east across the corner of a large field, and in 200 yards go through a narrow kissing gate in the fence. Now go due south across fields for ¼ mile, and eventually arrive on the lane through IFORD. Turn L and walk between flint walls and cottages to the parish church.

The church of St Nicholas is mainly Norman. It has a solid central tower with a shingled pyramid roof. Inside, notice especially the fine decoration on the semicircular arch between the nave and tower, the earliest part of the church.

Go L to continue along the lane through the village for another ¼ mile, turning R at a T-junction. After wet weather, stay on the road and at the main road turn L to walk to North-ease Farm. Otherwise, on reaching a sharp R bend, cross a stile ahead and turn L on a path along the east side of a large field. Now proceed south across the middle of this field, and after a further stile head across a sometimes swampy field to a kissing gate at its far corner.

Cross the main road and set off up the concrete track opposite, through Northease Farm. Pursue this as it heads first to the foot of the downs and then bears L to ascend once more to the South Downs Way. There are good views L to Lewes, Cliffe Hill and Mount Caburn, the levels around the river Ouse and bulky Beddingham Hill.

At the top of the climb pass through a small gate R and walk up the gently rising Way on its high ridge. Beyond another gate take up a concrete lane continuing over Front Hill and Iford Hill (600ft). When this leaves the South Downs Way follow it L to make for a prominent barn. Now unsurfaced, the track swings south along another ridge, with a prospect L to the white cliff of Seaford Head and the towns of Seaford, Newhaven and Peacehaven.

Nearly a mile after the barn, where the main path turns L at a field boundary, you must go R to descend steeply into the valley of Balsdean, with its pumping station L. Just beyond the lowest point go through a small gate and turn R along a flinty track towards distant Castle Hill. In about ½ mile you will arrive in a grove where many paths intersect at the foot of Bullock Hill. Follow the main track north to the farm buildings. Pass them L, and go through a gate to continue walking north, along the eastern side of the broad valley called Falmer Bottom. Bear L in front of a steep-sloped hill, and soon afterwards go through a small gate into the Castle Hill National Nature Reserve, which English Nature manages as a fine example of chalk downland. Keep going north as the path climbs the upper part of the valley, arriving at length on the South Downs Way.

Turn L, and after nearly a mile you will be back at the car park north of WOODINGDEAN where you started.

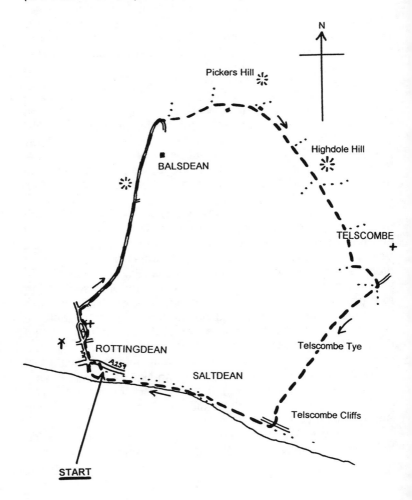

Pickers Hill

Highdole Hill

BALSDEAN

TELSCOMBE

ROTTINGDEAN

A259

SALTDEAN

Telscombe Tye

Telscombe Cliffs

START

Walk 32

BALSDEAN VALLEY

Rottingdean - Balsdean - Pickers Hill - Highdole Hill -
Telscombe Tye - Saltdean - Rottingdean

*A truly splendid ramble across rolling pastoral landscape, on mainly firm ground
and gentle gradients. It ends with a bracing stretch along the cliff tops or on the
undercliff promenade. There are pubs, cafes and toilets in Rottingdean and a
cafe and toilets on the Undercliff at Saltdean.*

Distance 7 miles   **Climbing** 800ft   **Highest point** 410ft

Start from the pay-and-display clifftop car park about 150
yards east of the ROTTINGDEAN crossroads on A259 *(map
ref TQ 372022).*

Turn L on leaving the car park, and at the traffic lights
go R up Rottingdean High Street, with its quaint old shops and
pubs. Cross Steyning Road, and then go R along Vicarage
Lane to pass the village pond and green L. If you have time,
pop in to the parish church.
*St Margaret's is a flint building with a Norman nave
and Early English chancel and central tower. Much of the
stained glass is by Sir Edward Burne-Jones, a famous resi-
dent of Rottingdean.*
After the church, keep walking north for about 300
yards, and turn R up Bazehill Road, which at first rises steeply
but soon leads on to the open downs. Continue along the
same lane as it becomes a private road to Balsdean farm and
pumping station, and look back for a good view over the sea
and the prominent black smock mill by the pitch and putt
course.
Pass the entrance drive to some tile-hung houses R,
and follow the same tarmac lane as it soon gently descends to
the lonely valley of BALSDEAN. Immediately beyond the
point where the road turns 180° to head for the pumping

station, take a track L, and in 40 yards go through a small wooden gate R. Now ascend a grassy path between fields on the western slopes of Pickers Hill, and go through another gate near the top.

In 200 yards bear R, pass a brick barn R, and in another 100 yards bear R again to pass another barn L. The walk continues south-east for about 1½ miles along a lofty ridge, passing close to the barely discernible summit of High-dole Hill L and the hump of a downland reservoir R. Notice the fine views, at first R into a valley with Saltdean at its mouth, then L to distant Mount Caburn, Beddingham Hill and Firle Beacon, with Seaford Head nearest the sea.

When the main track veers L, go through a small gate and carry straight on, south-easterly. After the first of two white houses R, bear L along a bridleway above the deep valley in which lies TELSCOMBE. In a further 500 yards arrive on a made up lane. If you have time, a visit to Tels-combe is an interesting diversion (*see Walk 33*).

Now turn R, and 30 yards on take the bridleway over Telscombe Tye, which was one of the ancient sheep downs of Sussex, now registered as common land. It now serves as an important green wedge in the built up areas of Saltdean and Peacehaven.

Walk seawards along this path for just over a mile until it joins the main coast road. Cross the road, and now walk along the clifftop down to SALTDEAN. Go L down the side road to find the toilets and seafront cafe. Then you have the choice of returning to ROTTINGDEAN either up the grass slope and along the clifftop or by the sheltered undercliff promenade.

Walk 33

SOUTHEASE AND THE OUSE

Saltdean - Telscombe Tye - Telscombe - Cricketing Bottom - Southease - Rodmell - Fore Hill - Highdole Hill - Pickers Hill Farm - Saltdean

A walk that is full of variety, with clifftops, hills, valleys, river bank, meadows and no less than three ancient and beautiful churches along the way. There's a pub/restaurant at Rodmell and a seafront cafe at Saltdean.

Distance 11½ miles   **Climbing** 730ft   **Highest point** 350ft

Start in the car park behind the SALTDEAN Lido *(map ref TQ 381021)* on the Brighton-Newhaven coast road.

Go south to the main road, cross it with care and turn L for a bracing short climb along the clifftops. About 100 yards after the last house in Saltdean cross the road again and take the path going north over Telscombe Tye, the green belt between Saltdean and Peacehaven.

On the crest of the hill, go straight on down the lane to TELSCOMBE. Walk past the front of the tiny youth hostel to visit the church of St Laurence.

Most of its fabric dates from the early Norman period, but the simple tower and north chapel were added about a century later. Inside it is rather dark, but there are interesting features, especially the Norman arches and piers.

Carry on down the road and then begin to climb past a flint building R with a round tower. When the lane bears R, take the bridleway L, going down into Cricketing Bottom. Mount Caburn, across the Ouse valley, beckons for most of the way, except when you pass through the farm where there is an old shepherd's hut R and a flint tithe barn L.

When the track swings L to meet the main road, take a path R, just below the road. Climb a small hill and emerge

MAP FOR WALK 33
(OS Pathfinder maps 1307 and 1308)

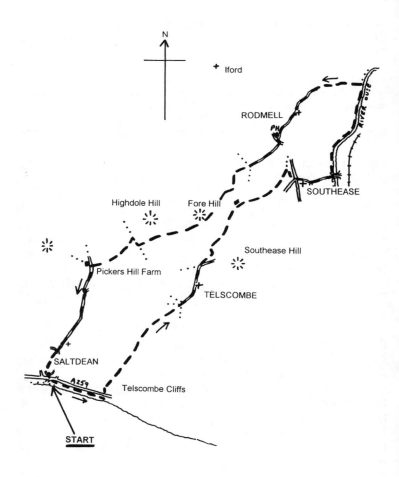

through a gate at a road junction. Walk south down the road for 50 yards and then turn L along the lane into SOUTHEASE.

The tiny, round-towered, Norman church here is light, welcoming and beautiful in its simplicity. It contains fine examples of Norman windows and traces of 13th century wall paintings.

Continue down the lane, and just before the narrow metal bridge over the Ouse take the path L and stay on the river bank for about a mile, enjoying the views ahead of Lewes and later Rodmell L, and Mount Caburn R.

Just before the river makes a sharp bend R, leave the bank for a track heading west across the meadows. At first it seems to be heading for Iford, but then it veers L and goes to the flint village of RODMELL. Just after passing Monks House, a National Trust property that was the home of Virginia and Leonard Woolf, go through a twitten L, and through the school playground to the church.

St Peter's is much darker than Southease church, but it is worth visiting to see fine examples of Norman work, especially in the carved arches. Here you may be able to buy an interesting guide to the village.

Go back to the village street and turn L. On reaching the main road at the Abergavenny Arms, cross it and walk straight up the lane opposite. This makes height quickly (in other words, it's steep!), and near the top gives a good view across the valley to the sea and Seaford Head.

At the top, go through the gate ahead and drop down into the valley, keeping a fence and bushes R. Follow the fence as it veers L at the bottom, and then climb out of the valley by a terraced footpath, now with a fence and bushes L. Go through a small wooden gate and continue up to the rounded top of Fore Hill. Note the vineyard in Breaky Bottom on your R.

Continue along a wide ridge between valleys, making for some bushes near the top of flat-topped Highdole Hill in the west. Keep the bushes and a fence R for 200 yards, and then go through a farm gate and carry on west across the field to emerge on a north-south bridleway. Turn R for about 20 yards and then go L along a muddy track into the valley where Saltdean comes into view. To the R are the valley of Balsdean and flat-topped Bullock Hill.

Descend to Pickers Hill Farm, where you must turn L along a track into the northern outskirts of SALTDEAN. Pass the tiny football ground R and head south all the way past St Nicholas's church L and across a green back to the car park.

The round-towered church at Southease *(Walk 33)*

Walk 34

PIDDINGHOE

Peacehaven - Lower Hoddern Farm - Nore Down - Piddinghoe
- Lodge Hill - Hoddern Farm - Peacehaven

An easy ramble over the downs to a picturesque riverside village with a Norman church and a half-way pub.

Distance 4 miles   **Climbing** 330ft   **Highest point** 230ft

Start at Lower Hoddern Farm, PEACEHAVEN, by parking in Pelham Rise or Glynn Road *(map ref TQ 417023)*.

Walk east through the farm, and in 300 yards turn R in front of a low flint wall. Walk down the track until the wall goes L. Now turn L to head east for over ½ mile, into a shallow valley and out the other side. Just below the top of a gorse-covered hill take a footpath L. Follow it as it bears R, but when it is joined by a south-north path turn L, and go over the little summit to the north.

Keep walking north along this ridge, Nore Down, with views to Lewes, Cliffe Hill and Beddingham Hill to the north, and South Heighton, Newhaven and Seaford Head to the east. The path descends to a farm and becomes a rough track that joins the main road at PIDDINGHOE. Cross the road and walk along a grass path to St John's church, with its golden fish weather-vane.

Piddinghoe's church, on a little hill above the Ouse, boasts one of the Ouse valley's three Norman round towers and some fine Norman arches inside. The Royal Oak pub is just down the road in front of the church gate.

Turn L out of the church gate and walk down to the river, where there are seats for picnickers. Walk by the river for 50 yards, and then follow the path inland. Arriving at the

MAP FOR WALK 34
(OS Pathfinder map 1308)

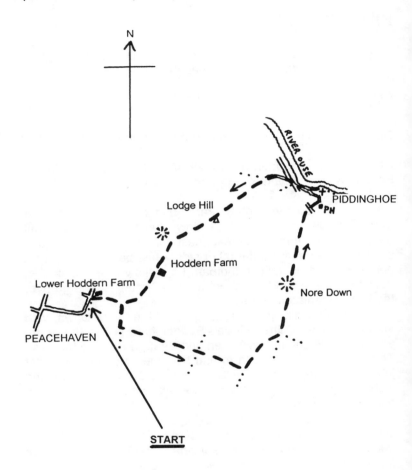

N

RIVER OUSE

Lodge Hill

PIDDINGHOE

PH

Hoddern Farm

Lower Hoddern Farm

Nore Down

PEACEHAVEN

START

old road through Piddinghoe turn R and walk on its R side. Joining the main road to Lewes continue north for only about 30 yards, and then cross to a surfaced bridleway heading up hill L.

Stay on this 'path' as it climbs steadily to a ridge over Lodge Hill, which is unusual in having a trig point well below the highest point. Pass through Hoddern Farm and arrive back at Lower Hoddern Farm, PEACEHAVEN, about 1½ miles after leaving Piddinghoe.

The river Ouse at Piddinghoe *(Walk 35)*

MAP FOR WALK 35
(OS Pathfinder map 1308)

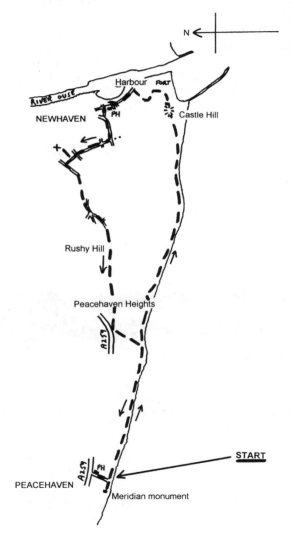

Walk 35

HARBOUR VIEW

Peacehaven - Harbour Heights - Castle Hill - Newhaven - Rushy Hill - Peacehaven

An airy stroll along the clifftops and a super view to end the book - but be very careful along the unfenced and crumbly cliff edge. Pubs at the start/finish point and at half way.

Distance 6 miles   **Climbing** 450ft   **Highest point** 250ft

Start at the Steyning Avenue car park on the South Coast Road at PEACEHAVEN, opposite the Dewdrop Inn *(map ref TQ 412009).*

Walk south down Steyning Avenue to the clifftop, where, if you have time, there is a way down to a short sea-front promenade. This walk, however, goes L along the clifftop path for about 2½ miles. Take great care because the cliff edge is unfenced after you leave the built up area.

Stay as close to the edge as you safely can, and as you approach a point above the harbour breakwater keep to the high ground. Pause on the concrete war-time fortifications next to the coastguard look-out and tall mast on CASTLE HILL, overlooking Newhaven Harbour.

Before about 1560 the town was called 'Meeching', but then the river Ouse, which had entered the sea further east at Seaford, cut a more direct way through and created a 'New Haven' here, below Castle Hill. There is a splendid view north of the harbour, with its marina and Channel ferry terminal and of South Heighton, backed by Beddingham Hill. To the east are Bishopstone and Seaford, with Windover Hill in the distance.

You may like to return to Peacehaven by the way you came, along the clifftop, this time taking in the view westward to Worthing and beyond. If, however, you prefer a change of scenery, go past the coastguard look-out on its seaward side and some more wartime defences L. Then turn L down hill for 10 yards and go R along a stony track that descends gently towards the harbour. Arriving at a car park turn L down a surfaced lane that curves R and passes a recreation ground L as you enter NEWHAVEN.

On reaching Fort Road that goes parallel with the river, turn L and pass the Sheffield Arms and the coastguard station L. Then go L up Geneva Road. In 100 yards fork L and go L again when this unmade road joins Hill Crest Road. Then take the next turning R, Second Avenue, which climbs steadily. Near the top a path R leads to St Michael's, the parish church of Newhaven, now used jointly by Anglicans and Methodists.

Newhaven church has a fine Norman central tower and apse, and a slightly later shingled broach spire. The rest of the building is comparatively modern. The interior is unusual in that the tower area serves as the chancel, and the altar is in the apse.

Continue to the end of Second Avenue and then turn L to pass the hospital R. Continue in the same direction as the road becomes a rough track and again when it is a footpath heading west along the south side of a grass area. At the end of this you will emerge on another unmade road called The Highway. Pass the BBC mast L and now walk west, past a large caravan park at Rushy Hill. Just before it joins the main road go L down a concrete road L. Now rejoin the cliff path that will take you right back to Steyning Avenue, PEACEHAVEN.

If you have time before going back to the car park, make the short diversion up the clifftop pavement to the King George V Monument, erected in 1936 on the line of the Greenwich Meridian. Read the inscription on the north side, to find the number of miles and degrees from places all round the world.

Chalk cliffs at Saltdean *(Walk 32)*

A SUSSEX GLOSSARY

For people unfamiliar with the way we talk in south Sussex, here is a translation of some of the terms used in this book.

Bottom   A valley.

Coombe   A usually steep hollow in the hills.

Dewpond   A circular pond artificially created on the downs to catch and hold rain water for farm animals.

Downs   Why are our hills called 'downs' when you have to climb up? Because the word is derived from the Saxon 'dun', meaning a hill!

Kissing gate A gate that enables only one person to pass through before admitting the next. Named because the first expects a kiss before allowing the second to pass through.

Reservoir   On the downs all reservoirs are under ground; all you see above ground is a grass-covered mound that looks something like the bottom part of a pyramid.

Staddle stones Mushroom shaped stones, used to support a granary or other building that needs to stand clear of the ground.

Tapsell gate A gate that works on the principle of the revolving door. It turns on a spindle at the centre.

Twitten   A narrow passage between houses (alley, loke, snicket, gant in other parts of England)

KEY TO MAPS

- →- - -	route of walk
(roads lines)	roads and lanes
· · · · · · ·	other paths & bridleways
+-+-+-+-+-+-+	railways
Δ	triangulation point (trig point)
(hillfort symbol)	hillfort
(hill top symbol)	hill top
+	church
Ӿ	windmill
■	other building
PH	public house
CH	golf club house

METRIC CONVERSION

Britain is gradually becoming more used to metric measurements. For example, Ordnance Survey maps now use metres for heights, including hill tops and contours. However, the highway authorities still use miles to measure road distances, so we are stuck with a confusing compromise.

For the sake of consistency in this book, I have kept to 'Imperial' measures - miles, yards and feet - for both heights and distances. The following chart should help when you need to translate Imperial to Metric or Metric to Imperial.

HEIGHT DISTANCE

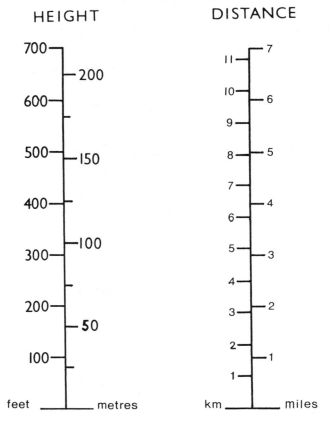

INDEX TO PLACES VISITED

Ovingdean	29,30	Stanmer	26
Patcham	25	Stanmer Park	26,27
Patching	3	Steep Down	14
Peacehaven	34,35	Steyning	12,13,16
Perching Hill	20	Steyning Bowl	13
Perry Hill	1	Steyning Round Hl	12,13
Pickers Hill	32	Streat Hill	28
Piddinghoe	34	Stretham Manor	16
Plumpton Plain	28	Sullington & Hill	6
Poling	2	Swanborough	31
Poynings	22,23	Sweet Hill	25
Pyecombe	24,25	Telscombe	33
Rackham Hill	1	Telscombe Tye	32,33
Red Hill	29	Tenants Hill	11
Rodmell	33	Thundersbarrow	20
Rottingdean	29,32	Truleigh Hill	16,20
Rushy Hill	35	Upper Beeding	15,16
Saddlescombe	23	Washington	6,7,12
Saltdean	32,33	Wepham	1
Shoreham airport	17	West Hill, Findon	8
Small Dole	16	West Hill, N'timber	23,25
Sompting	11	West Kingston	5
Soper's Bottom	13	Wild Park	27
Southease	33	Windmill Hill	15
South Stoke	1	Wiston House	12
Southwick Hill	19,20	Wolstonbury Hill	24,25
Springhead Hill	1	Woodingdean	30,31